Beacon
STREET

Beacon
STREET
Its Buildings & Residents

Robert E. Guarino

Charleston · London

THE
History
PRESS

Published by The History Press
Charleston, SC 29403
www.historypress.net

Back cover: The Boston Athenaeum building at 10½ Beacon Street in 1902.
Courtesy the Boston Athenaeum.

First published 2011

Manufactured in the United States

ISBN 978.1.60949.124.6

Library of Congress Cataloging-in-Publication Data

Guarino, Robert E.
Beacon Street : its buildings and residents / Robert E. Guarino.
p. cm.
ISBN 978-1-60949-124-6
1. Beacon Street (Boston, Mass.)--History. 2. Historic buildings--Massachusetts--Boston. 3.
Architecture--Massachusetts--Boston--History. 4. Beacon Street (Boston, Mass.)--Buildings,
structures, etc. 5. Boston (Mass.)--Buildings, structures, etc. 6. Beacon Street (Boston,
Mass.)--Biography. 7. Boston (Mass.)--Biography. 8. Boston (Mass.)--History. I. Title.
F73.67.B43G83 2011
974.4'61--dc22
2011000062

For Gerry

CONTENTS

Preface

When I lived on Beacon Street between 1982 and 2003 and walked in the area, it was inevitable that on almost every excursion I would be stopped by a tourist or visitor and asked for directions to this place or that and often questioned about who lived in the particular building in front of which we had stopped. Only a few of the structures along the section of Beacon Street that runs beside Beacon Hill and its "flats" had tablets or signs indicating some prominent personage or an event that had happened there or near there, and I was often stumped and unable to give a response when queried about different addresses.

It was after ten years of living on Beacon Street and encountering these visitors that I decided to try to research the very structures with which I had become so familiar, starting with my own residence in an 1850s brownstone and brick building at 90 Beacon.

I decided to trace back the ownership of the buildings and the ownership of early structures that may have been at the same locations, as well as the ownership of the land on which the structures were built, all the way back to the original settlers of Boston and their rights to the original land.

At about the same time, I learned about the existence of insurance atlases that had been printed in the nineteenth and twentieth centuries and accurately displayed a footprint of every building along the street, as well as the names of the owners in the respective years of the atlases. This information, along with my desire to know who had owned and lived in the respective buildings, led me on a research project that I found more interesting the further back in history I went.

I discovered that the original ownership of the Shawmut Peninsula surely rested with the Native Americans who resided here probably for millennia and used the shores for fishing during the summer months. The people who lived in the area were of the Massachusett tribe, of Algonquin stock, when William Blackstone first came here in 1624.

The purpose of this book is to provide the reader with an understanding of the unique history of Beacon Street and its past and present residents and property owners, commencing with the initial possession of the land by Native Americans and followed by the English exploration of the area and eventual settlement by the first European, William Blackstone. The story continues until the 1950s, when changes to the buildings and homes essentially stopped, with the exception of One Beacon Street, an office building that was added in the 1970s.

While they were built primarily as single-family dwellings, sometimes referred to as dwelling houses, the use of the various homes changed throughout the succeeding decades. Also described herein are mansion houses, free-standing dwellings unattached to their neighbors; and row houses, single-family homes of similar, if not identical, design that were attached to others either in double, triple or larger form or sometimes as mirror images of the adjacent house.

After the population migration to the suburban lifestyle in the early twentieth century, many houses were sold to businesspeople, who changed the use to apartment houses, and many became rooming houses as well. It wasn't until the 1960s and 1970s that people started returning to the city, and the popularity of condominiums created the opportunity to live an affordable city life with home ownership.

Walking Beacon Street from Tremont to Arlington Streets gives people today a rare chance to see the eighteenth, nineteenth and twentieth centuries come alive. The beautiful red brick town houses and Charles Bullfinch's splendid 1798 statehouse grace one of America's most historic streets, which, along with the Boston Common and Public Garden, allows for rare panoramic views of the unique lineup of architecture.

The part of Beacon Street that I am writing about contains the area starting from present-day Tremont Street west over Beacon Hill, past the statehouse, down to Charles Street and on to the "flat of the hill" to where 99 Beacon Street once existed, approximately opposite the northern end of Arlington Street. This book is, in fact, a genealogy of the street that enables the reader, when observing today's buildings and landscape, to discover the history of each present-day address. Also referenced are now nonexistent addresses and their respective structures, along with chapters on groups or events that markedly influenced the scenes we see on Beacon Street today.

This book can be used as a visitors' guide, accompanying one on a sort of traveler's sojourn through time. It should also appeal to scholars and residents who are fascinated by the historical sights before them and have an interest in discovering their past.

Included are brief biographies of many of the notables who lived on the street and many photographs, engravings and maps relating to the addresses.

The introduction describes the reasons for the Massachusetts Bay Company's decision to settle in Boston and outlines how the town grew around the harbor and Blackstone's residence. The subsequent chapters show the history of addresses, both no longer extant and still existing, and the progression of ownership of those sites and buildings.

Much of the material gathered here is from research done at the primary level at the Suffolk County Registry of Deeds (SRD) and at the secondary level in many books and files, both written and illustrative, from various repositories, including, but not limited to, the Boston Athenaeum, Historic New England (SPNEA), the Bostonian Society, the John F. Kennedy Library and the Massachusetts Historical Society. The assistance of the staffs at these venerable institutions has been greatly appreciated. I also offer special thanks to Jack Leonard, without whose constant reviewing, correcting and encouragement this book would never have happened.

Many of the very early references to land ownership are derived from the *Fifth Report of the Record of Commissioners* printed in Boston in 1880. As described in the preface to that volume, written by William H. Whitmore and William S. Appleton, commissioners, the report "contains a series of articles relating to the history of estates lying on or around Beacon Hill. These articles were contributed in 1855 to the *Boston Daily Transcript* by the late Nathaniel Ingersoll Bowditch, under the signature of 'Gleaner.'"

Mr. Bowditch, a prominent conveyancer of his day, goes into great detail about land ownership from the very first ownership of William Blackstone up until the approximate time of the publication of his articles in the *Boston Daily Transcript*. His descriptions of the owners are not only informative but also, in many cases, humorous. I have included his title research in many of my addresses and have expanded on them where necessary to bring my book up to the 1950s. I refer to his writings in my notes as "Gleaner."

Notes on the Images

Many of the structures included here have remained virtually unchanged externally from the time they were first built, a few in the eighteenth century and many in the early and mid-nineteenth century. In these cases, I have provided images of either the earliest photographs or the most current for almost all the addresses. In instances where a house or building no longer exists, or if there have been substantial changes to its appearance, more than one image is provided to show evolution and change.

When looking at the images in this history, we are imagining a perspective from the center of Beacon Street when considering addresses between Tremont Street and Park Street. Between Park Street and Arlington Street, we are imagining a view from the Boston Common or the Public Garden, looking northward toward Beacon Street.

Images with more than one address should be read from left to right; that is, when multiple dwellings appear in the same image, the one to the far left will be the highest number, while the far right will be the lowest, unless otherwise noted. Additionally, if there is a partial image of an address, generally it is not included in the caption.

Image captions list the source with a courtesy reference. Photographs not credited were either taken by me or are from my collection.

INTRODUCTION

S tanding in front of the venerable King's Chapel and Burying Ground—the "old burial place"—on Tremont Street and looking westward up Beacon Street, one cannot easily imagine how that vista has changed since the Puritans settled Boston in 1630.

When the Reverend William Blackstone, the first European to settle in what was then known by the Massachusett Indians as Shawmut (the Place of Living Fountains), arrived here in 1624, the land was similar in appearance to what you might find today on some Boston Harbor islands. The topography consisted of sandy bluffs reaching down to the shore, with marshes and many low shrubs, including wild roses, blueberry and barberry bushes. Native trees of pine, maple and birch were scarce, as was meadowland, while red cedar and oak trees prevailed.

In addition, there were many freshwater springs on the peninsula, both near the sea and on the hillsides. These springs were the main reason that Governor John Winthrop's fledgling Massachusetts Bay Company accepted, in 1630, the invitation of Blackstone to settle here. It was not long after their arrival on Shawmut—or Trimontaine (Treamont, Tramount), as it has been called—that the court of assistants, with Winthrop presiding, ordered "that Trimontaine shall be called Boston."[1]

Boston's famous poet Oliver Wendell Holmes aptly described the area in the poem "Boston Common: Three Pictures," written "for the Fair in aid of the fund to procure Ball's statute of Washington," which stands at the Commonwealth Avenue entrance to the Public Garden:

Trimontaine.

1630

All overgrown with bush and fern,
And straggling clumps of tangled trees,
With trunks that lean and boughs that turn,
Bent eastward by the mastering breeze,-
With spongy bogs that drip and fill
A yellow pond with muddy rain,
Beneath the shaggy southern hill
Lies wet and low the Shawmut plain.
And hark! The trodden branches crack;
A crow flaps off with startled scream;
A straying woodchuck canters back;
A bittern rises from the stream;
Leaps from his lair a frightened deer;
An otter plunges in the pool,-
Here comes old Shawmut's pioneer,
The parson on his brindled bull.

Introduction

When Blackstone first came, there were most likely paths through Shawmut created by the indigenous Massachusett Indians and animals going to their hunting grounds or drinking places. At the most favorable location, Blackstone constructed a house for himself. The exact location of the house is unknown, but it was probably in the vicinity of 50 Beacon Street, where there were known to be natural springs and where the land was high enough to avoid any flooding from the Charles River. So here we have the first house erected on the Shawmut Peninsula. It was many years before others decided to move to the far western part of the peninsula.

When John Winthrop first visited the Shawmut Peninsula from Charlestown, he and his party arrived in a small boat in order to navigate the shallow Charles River and landed on the beach west of Blackstone's house in an area later known as Blackstone's Point. Due to the tidal nature of the Charles River, however, that landing area was not safe for ships the size of the *Lady Arbella*, on which the new arrivals had crossed the Atlantic Ocean. Hence, the colonists chose to erect their houses near the town cove, with its deep-water anchorages for their ships.

Blackstone must have utilized some of the ancient paths to reach various parts of the peninsula, as most of the hills were covered with brambles and bushes, making walking difficult if not impossible. To reach what was to become the town cove, he would have walked along the edge of the Common, as that was where the hills flattened out and he could ride his bull on fairly level ground. Thus was the beginning of Beacon Street.

As we can see, it was already necessary for travelers between Blackstone's home and the settlement to use the pathway between the east and west sides of Shawmut. In 1635, the pathway was further enhanced by the issuance of an order authorizing the erection of a beacon atop the adjacent Centry Hill to warn inhabitants of danger or invasion and a subsequent order to keep the path open to the beacon. The hill was to become known by its current name of Beacon Hill, and the lane was called Beacon Street.

1

WILLIAM BLACKSTONE

William Blackstone (also Blaxton), the first European inhabitant of Boston, arrived in New England in 1623 with Robert Gorges, who had received a grant from the Council of New England in 1622 and had been sent to Massachusetts Bay to settle in the area of the new state encompassed by his grant. Robert was the son of Sir Ferdinando Gorges, one of the principal adventurers (shareholders) of the council.

His contingent settled in Wessagusset (Weymouth) in an outpost that had been abandoned by Thomas Weston from the Pilgrim colony in Plymouth. Gorges was soon discouraged with the enterprise and returned to England the following year. He left behind a number of settlers, including Blackstone, who decided instead to remain in the New World and discover a place where he could live without the religious pressure of his fellow settlers.

Blackstone, an ordained minister, eventually settled on the Shawmut Peninsula in 1624[2] and claimed title to the peninsula, as he was the first white settler and the sole English inhabitant until 1630. During that time, he built a modest house on the west side of Beacon Hill at the site of a spring of fresh water that was believed to be in the vicinity of today's 50 Beacon Street. He started an apple orchard, some of whose trees were still bearing fruit one hundred years later.[3] He also tended his cattle, cared for his rose garden and spent much time reading books and occasionally trading with the Indians.

In June 1630, Winthrop's fleet arrived at the "City upon a Hill," the Salem settlement, eager to explore the New World. Winthrop's group, the Massachusetts Bay Company, had received a patent from the Crown that

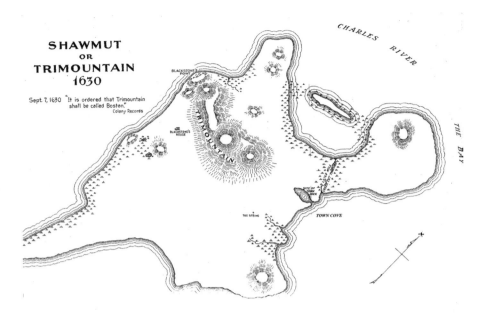

A 1630 map of Shawmut showing Blackstone's house and the town cove.

essentially covered much of the same area that Gorges had been granted and led to Ferdinando Gorges's long fight to have the company's charter declared invalid.

The Salem area, however, was not acceptable to the new settlers, and within five days they set out exploring for a more suitable location, with Winthrop eventually locating in Charlestown. This setting also did not prove satisfactory as some disliked the physical location and others were apprehensive that the French might attack them. The French, old foes, were claiming that the English were settling in territories where the French had settled first and therefore had rights of ownership. A decision was made to disperse the settlement; some settlers set up bases in Mattapan, Watertown and Roxbury, while Winthrop's group stayed in Charlestown until the lack of decent drinking water became so acute that it was necessary for them to find another home.

One of the settlers accompanying Winthrop was Isaac Johnson, a minister and an Emmanuel College classmate of William Blackstone. Blackstone, upon learning of Johnson's arrival, invited him and then Winthrop and his group, to visit Tramount, as Shawmut was first called. Learning of

The Founders Memorial, honoring Boston's first settlers, shows William Blackstone welcoming John Winthrop to Shawmut. The memorial was erected on Boston Common in 1930 for the tercentenary celebration of Boston's original settlement. John Paramino was the sculptor.

their privations in Charlestown, Blackstone urged them to come and live at Shawmut, as there were many springs and the area already had many clearings for houses and gardens, making it an easy place to start a settlement. Winthrop and many other settlers, including Johnson and John Wilson, another minister, accepted the invitation, and on September 7, 1630, the Massachusetts Bay Company settlement of Tramount welcomed settlers, goods and the charter.

In 1631, Blackstone, who was considered by the colonists to be one of the "Old Planters" that included Samuel Maverick from Gorges's party and others such as Wollaston, Morton and Weston,[4] was admitted to the colony as a freeman, giving him rights of citizenship, including the right to vote.

As the settlement grew, many of the colonists thought that they should assert their rights under the charter to, in effect, be able to grant lands as they saw appropriate. The question of whether Blackstone actually had legal title to all the land was never explicitly documented by Winthrop, but the fact that they granted him land equal to almost 7 percent of the entire Shawmut Peninsula shows that they were trying to prevent any disagreements with him.

He "may have possessed Shawmut by lease or purchase from Gorges… This is extremely probable," [5] as Blackstone was not driven off his land by the Massachusetts Bay Company when it later asserted its rights under the charter because of his hospitality to the colonists and because he was settled on his claim. However, within three years the new Massachusetts colony would proceed to evict him from his property.

In 1633, the Massachusetts Bay Company exercised its right of ownership to the land described in its charter, including the Shawmut Peninsula, which Blackstone claimed. On April 1, the general court set aside fifty acres for Blackstone, including the area under his house.

On October 9, 1634, Blackstone sold his interest in the Shawmut Peninsula and all rights to "any of the lands lying within the said neck called Boston"[6] for thirty pounds; he also sold off forty-four of the fifty acres, much of which was to remain common land for the inhabitants and later became today's Boston Common. He retained the six acres on which sat his house, garden and orchard.

The colony now felt confident of its ownership of Shawmut, and that fact, along with its charter provisions, enabled it to distribute land as it wished. This was recorded in the Boston Town Records of March 1636.

Although Sir Ferdinando Gorges and his heirs continued to dispute the legitimacy of the colonists' title to the Shawmut Peninsula, their legal ownership was not seriously questioned by the Crown until fifty years later, when again arose the issue of whether Blackstone's claim to Shawmut was valid. The charter problem was once again becoming an issue for the colony, and this time its validity was being tested by the Crown, which vacated the original charter in 1684.

Although the original charter had been vacated and a new one issued by the Crown, the actions of the Massachusetts Bay Company were never reversed by England, and the independence shown by the residents of Massachusetts manifested itself almost a century before the Battle of Lexington. As George Chalmers states in his 1780 *Political Annals*, when the citizens were defying some of the Crown's orders in 1677, "thus we hear for the first time…that the colonists, though in the same breath swearing allegiance to the Crown of England, were not bound by the Acts of Parliament, because they were not represented in it."

In 1634, Blackstone moved from Boston to Rhode Island, and sometime before 1655[7] he sold the Boston six-acre plot to Richard Pepys. In Rhode Island, he lived at a place called Study Hill, where he built a house on a site near what is now the Blackstone River. He returned to Boston numerous times, probably in his ecclesiastical role, and in 1665 married a widow, Sarah Stevenson, whom he brought to Rhode Island, to what is now Cumberland. They had one child, John.

Blackstone lived in Rhode Island until his death in 1675 at the age of eighty. His extensive library, which undoubtedly contained much information about the early days of Boston, was tragically burned, along with his house, during King Philip's War (1675–76).

In the 1877 *Second Report of the Record Commissioners* of the City of Boston, there is a transcription of records from the "Book of Possessions" describing owners of property from as early as 1645. This transcription includes Richard Pepys.

Richard Pepys bought Blackstone's reservation of six acres and built a house on it. William Pollard occupied the house for nearly fourteen years, during which time Blackstone "frequently resorted to it" on his visits from Rhode Island, as Anne Pollard deposed in 1711.

Gleaner traced this descent of the lot in 1828 and printed the story in the *Boston Courier*. It was repeated in the *Transcript* in 1855. The lot was later part of the estate of John Singleton Copley, the artist, and from him passed to the Mount Vernon Proprietors.

2

BEACON HILL

In 1624, as seen by William Blackstone, the most noticeable natural prominences of the Shawmut Peninsula, the area that was to become the town of Boston, were the three hills later named Beacon Hill, Fort Hill and Copp's Hill. Beacon Hill had three components, which "gave to it its first name Treamount"[8] (also Tramont), consisting of what were eventually called Mt. Vernon, Cotton Hill (also Pemberton Hill) and, most noticeably, Sentry (or Centry) Hill.[9] Sentry Hill, or as it was alternately and more famously known, Beacon Hill, had a summit that would have risen to just below the golden dome of today's Massachusetts Statehouse.[10] The name of Sentry Hill was used until the town ordained, in 1635,[11] the erection of a beacon on six square rods[12] of land on its summit to warn inhabitants of danger or invasion. Thus it became known by its current name, Beacon Hill.

The original beacon pole was a tall stick-like structure with an iron skillet on top that was full of combustibles that could be lit to warn the townspeople. The British took it down in 1775. After the British evacuation in 1776, the pole was erected again and stayed in place until 1789, when it was blown down by a severe storm.

In 1790, a project was started to replace the pole with a sturdy monument to commemorate events of the American Revolution. Charles Bulfinch was the architect of the column, which was made of stucco-covered bricks and topped with a large gilt eagle. The base was composed of four panels, each engraved with inscriptions—two commemorating the important events of the Revolution, and two dedicated to the citizens of Boston and all Americans.

An engraving by Bowen showing Beacon Hill's three components: Pemberton Hill (also called Cotton Hill), Mt. Vernon and Beacon Hill.

The cutting down of Beacon Hill, showing the 1791 Bulfinch Monument and the north side of the Massachusetts Statehouse. From an 1811 drawing by J.R. Smith. *Courtesy of the Boston Athenaeum.*

This column stood until 1811, when the Town of Boston, in desperate financial need, decided to sell off some of its town lands. The six square rods on which the column sat were sold to a group that included John Hancock, nephew of the late governor, and Samuel Spear, a relation of the nephew's through marriage. The new owners, after dismantling the Bulfinch monument, proceeded to dig down the hill in order to sell the valuable gravel beneath the surface (see section on the Daniel Dennison Rogers Estate). This reduced the height of Beacon Hill to its current level.

Fortunately, the four tablets at the base of the monument were retained and stored in the basement of the statehouse. They were later reinstalled on a new monument that exists today on the east side of the Charles E. Brigham addition, added in 1895.

3

TREMONT STREET TO SOMERSET STREET

North Side

ONE BEACON

It is certain that the early settlers of Boston could never have imagined the building that today sits at the northwest corner of Beacon and Tremont Streets. This pink polished granite structure is the latest in a series of houses, hotels and business buildings that have stood here since the early seventeenth century.

The house and land at the corner of those two streets would have first belonged to James Penn, one of the first settlers in Boston. He owned the property as early as 1658, and there he built his "dwelling-house."[13] Penn had either been granted this land or had purchased it from the adjacent landowners, John Wilson or John Coggan (see section on the Tremont Building).

Penn had accompanied John Winthrop's Massachusetts Bay Company settlers, who arrived Boston in 1630. He was named messenger of the general court (today's state legislature) in 1634 and was elected selectman of the town of Boston in 1636. In 1645, he was town clerk and treasurer. Penn also became beadle of the First Church, of which he later became a ruling elder, and in 1648 the people of Boston elected him deputy to the general court.

In 1671, Penn bequeathed the property to his nephew, Colonel Penn Townsend, including his dwelling house and land that extended up Beacon Street 150 feet to James Allen's land. Colonel Townsend had, at various times, been both a representative and deputy to the general court. He attained the rank of colonel in the Boston militia and was on a committee appointed to fortify the town against what many perceived to be an imminent invasion

One Beacon Street, a thirty-seven-floor office building built in 1974 and designed by Skidmore, Owings and Merrill.

of Boston by the French. He was also elected as deputy to the last session of the general court in 1686 and under the new legislative system was elected Speaker of the lower house. After retiring, he became a successful wine merchant and left a considerable fortune.

His executor sold the property in 1750 to Samuel Sturgis, and by 1784 the land and buildings were owned by Samuel Eliot, a wealthy Boston merchant and owner of a dry goods shop, who retained his well-known mansion house estate and gardens for many years. As Bowditch states in his Gleaner articles, "It embraced the Albion [hotel] and the block of brick houses west of it."[14]

Eliot was the father of Samuel Atkins Eliot, mayor of Boston (1837–39), and William H. Eliot, the developer of the adjacent Tremont House Hotel. Eliot's house, which is shown on Boynton's map of 1835, is a three-story wooden structure that was occupied by his widow for nine years after his death in 1820.

Following Eliot's wife's demise, the estate was sold in 1833 to Israel Thorndike, a developer of the times, who also was involved in the disposition of the John Hancock estate. Thorndike divided up the estate, creating lots on Beacon Street numbered two, three, four and five, on which were built dwelling houses. One Beacon, the prize portion at the corner of Beacon and Tremont Streets, Thorndike sold in 1836 to Francis Olmsted. This parcel included both land and the new Albion Hotel recently erected by Thorndike on that corner.

Olmsted in turn sold the property, in 1845, to John L. Gardner, one of the last of the East India merchants. The hotel was known as an apartment

Above: From an 1835
Boynton map of
Boston, showing a
Tremont Street scene
with the Eliot House
at the near right and
King's Chapel on
the left.

Right: Albion Hotel,
circa 1871. *Courtesy
of the Bostonian
Society/Old State
House Museum.*

hotel and was primarily for long-term residents, similar to today's apartment houses, and not for overnight guests.

The Albion was razed in 1888 and replaced by a nine-story office and professional building.

> *While there will be many regrets at the demolition of the Albion, there is some satisfaction in knowing that the building to be erected on its site will be in the line of improvement which has characterized the new structure recently constructed in the neighborhood. The corner location, with its abundance of light and air, offers facilities for a building which shall not be dwarfed even by the lofty Parker House near by. While it is to be regretted that King's Chapel will be greatly overtopped by the new structure, that historic pile has associations enough to maintain its dignity even in the face of the imposing "palace" of trade which Messrs. Houghton & Dutton are to erect on the site of the "Albion."*[15]

This new building, known as the Albion Building, was erected in 1888 by the estate of John Gardner and was designed by Cummins & Sears, architects.

Albion Building, 1895. *Courtesy of the Bostonian Society/ Old State House Museum.*

One of its primary tenants was the dry goods firm of Houghton & Dutton, one of the first department stores in the nation. The firm was very successful and continued to expand, eventually occupying and purchasing 1–5 Beacon, as well as 7 Beacon, the headquarters of the American Congregational Association.

In 1904, the Houghton & Dutton Department Store erected a new nine-story building designed by architects Horace Burr and Lyman Sise on land that covered an area that had formerly composed the estates of Penn and Reverend James Allen, from

28

Tremont Street to Somerset Streets, and all the land fronting on Beacon Street, a sizable building in all. In 1936, Houghton & Dutton went into receivership, and the property was taken over by the City of Boston, which rented it out to various government agencies, including the Veterans Administration.

In 1963, the vacant building was sold at auction to the real estate firm of Cabot, Cabot & Forbes. Two years later, the building was razed, and the area was used as a parking lot until 1969. After 242 years, one of the most important places in the history of Beacon Street and Beacon Hill was back to being an open space. Wouldn't the Puritans be surprised!

Houghton & Dutton Department Store, 1930. The store encompassed the entire block along Beacon Street from Tremont to Somerset Street. *Courtesy of Historic New England.*

But the airy spot was not long open. In 1969, the property was sold, and by 1974 the polished pink granite Employer's Building was erected as the United States headquarters for the London-based Employer's Commercial Union Insurance Company. The building was designed by Skidmore, Owings & Merrill and now "overtopped" the King's Chapel by thirty-seven stories. Another surprise to our predecessors! This edifice exists today as it did in 1974.

2 BEACON

The house originally constructed here was erected on land that was part of the Samuel Eliot estate purchased in 1833 by Israel Thorndike. Thorndike subsequently divided the estate into lots, with this parcel being sold in 1835 to Hersey and Caleb Stowell.

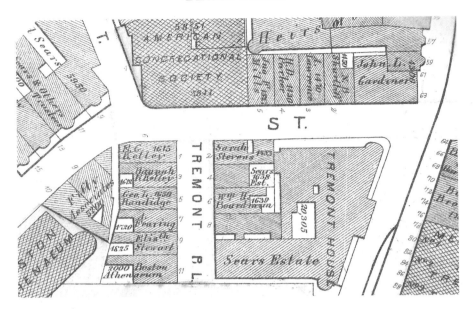

An 1874 Bromley insurance map showing 2, 3, 4 and 5 Beacon Street, as well as the Tremont House Hotel, Tremont Place and adjacent houses.

The Stowells erected a house probably designed by Cornelius Coolidge and sold the property the following year, 1836, to Dr. Nathaniel Bradstreet Shurtleff, physician, noted historian and mayor of Boston from 1868 to 1870. Shurtleff wrote the *Topographical and Historical Description of Boston*, published in 1871, an early comprehensive and authoritative history of the city of Boston. As mayor, he widened and extended the streets in the business section of the city, including the formation of Atlantic Avenue, which was constructed on top of the site of the seventeenth-century "barricado," a sunken barricade created to deter invasion of the city from the sea. He also was responsible for building a number of bridges and instituting the ferry service from Boston to East Boston, service that continued until the 1950s. It was also under his administration that Dorchester was annexed to Boston.

In 1878, the house was sold by the family to Harriet A. Lowell and was converted to professional offices. In 1909, her estate sold the building to the Houghton & Dutton Department Store, which utilized it as part of its store. In 1913, the house, along with 3 Beacon, was replaced with the expanding Houghton & Dutton building which eventually encompassed the entire block along Beacon from Tremont to Somerset Streets.

The sites of 1–5 and 7 Beacon are now part of One Beacon Street, and their numbers are no longer being used as addresses by the City of Boston.

3 Beacon

The house originally at this site was built on the Samuel Eliot estate purchased by Israel Thorndike and sold in 1835 to Joseph Lincoln.

In 1836, Lincoln erected a house probably designed by Cornelius Coolidge and sold the property the same year to Daniel Safford, blacksmith. Safford manufactured one of the first hot-air furnaces in this country, whose design is attributed to Solomon Willard, the "father of the granite industry."[16] After several owners, the house was purchased in 1862 by Gardiner Howland Shaw, who by 1865 had turned the property into a boardinghouse.

Thereafter, there were many businesses in the building, and in 1867 the Shaw estate sold it to Abbott Lawrence, a very successful businessman whose family helped found the city of Lawrence. Lawrence sold it in 1883 to H.H. Carter of the paper firm H.H. Carter Co.

The property remained an office building until 1909, when it was sold to the Houghton & Dutton Co.

4 Beacon

The house that was originally constructed here was built on one of five lots created by Israel Thorndike from the Samuel Eliot estate in 1833. Thorndike sold this property in 1835 to Loyal Lovejoy, owner of L. Lovejoy and Co., a lumber supply company located on Causeway Street in Boston and an officer in Blackstone Bank.

In 1836, Lovejoy sold the land and a house, which was probably designed and built by Cornelius Coolidge, to Adeline Burr. In 1853, the house belonged to Esther and Wharton J. Greene, who sold it in 1865 to the estate of Gardiner Howland Shaw, which also owned 3 Beacon. In 1868, the building was sold to Harvey D. Parker, creator of the Parker House Hotel.

Parker continued to use the building as offices and had as a tenant in 1880 the American Baptist Publishing Society. In 1885, Julia D. Parker sold the building to Francis Baker and the Richard Baker estate, which had as tenants the Houghton & Dutton Department Store and the Suffolk Club, a social club that counted among its members many prominent Democrats of the time.[17] The Imperial Club replaced the Suffolk Club in 1904, when the Suffolk moved to 3 Beacon.

In 1909, the Baker estate sold the building to the Houghton & Dutton Department Store, which demolished it (along with 5 Beacon) and replaced both with a new building.

5 BEACON

The house originally existing here was built on one of the five lots created by Israel Thorndike from the Samuel Eliot estate. It was sold in 1835 to Cornelius Coolidge, a well-known architect and building contractor.

Coolidge was involved in developing subdivided lots with Thorndike in different areas of Beacon Hill, and it is not unreasonable to assume that he was the architect and builder of 2–5 Beacon. In 1836, Coolidge sold the land, plus the house he had built on it, to John C. Proctor of Proctor & Clark, booksellers, and by 1849 the house belonged to Edwin Lamson.

In 1868, Lamson, a merchant with Twombly & Lamson of Central Wharf, sold to John F. Mills, who was employed by the Parker House.

In 1880, Mills was renting the building to the Houghton & Dutton Department Store, and in 1908 his estate sold the property to that company, which, in 1909, demolished the building, along with 4 Beacon, and replaced both with a new structure that was an addition to 7 Beacon.

7 BEACON

The Reverend James Allen owned the original house at this address. The property bordered James Penn's land on the east and continued along Beacon Street until it reached present-day Somerset Street on its western side. Allen owned the land as early as 1670 and built a stone house that was thought to be the first one erected in Boston.

Allen was installed as a minister of the First Church in 1668 and remained in that position for over forty years. Upon his death, his property was left to his son, Jeremiah, and subsequently to his grandson James, who sold it in 1789 to his brother, Jeremiah Allen, the high sheriff of Suffolk County. Jeremiah was sheriff under Governor John Hancock in 1792 and was the last to enforce the prohibition of theater plays being performed in Boston under the statute against thespianism that was rescinded by the general court on the last day of that year. Hence, one more of the state's early Puritan laws was struck down as a result of an increasingly sophisticated populace's demand.

Sheriff Allen died in 1809, and his heirs sold the estate in 1810 to David Hinckley. Hinckley tore down the original stone house and prepared to replace it with two connected stone houses set back from the street to be made of new stone and imported glass. The War of 1812 and the ensuing

Number 7 Beacon Street, the David Hinckley House (right), and 1 Somerset Street (left), circa 1860, later home of the Somerset Club.

economic downturn interrupted the construction of these houses, and it wasn't until 1820 that they were completed.

Benjamin Wiggins purchased the easterly house, 7 Beacon, from Hinckley in 1820, and in 1828 the house belonged to Joseph Peabody. Peabody purchased the house for his daughter, Catherine Elizabeth, who married John L. Gardner. They were the parents of John Lowell Gardner, who later married Isabella "Belle" Stewart in 1860. She was the creator of the famed Venetian home that today exists on the Fenway and is known as Fenway Court. Built as her home, it later became the Isabella Stewart Gardner Museum, one of Boston's most visited sites. Gardner's estate sold 7 Beacon to the American Congregational Association in 1871.

Mr. Hinckley occupied the westerly house, 1 Somerset Street, during his lifetime, and in 1826 the property was transferred to his daughter, Anne Outram Hinckley, and William G. Hodgkinson. In 1832, Benjamin W. Crowninshield, who had served as secretary of the navy under Presidents James Madison and James Monroe, purchased the house. Crowninshield also served in the United States Congress from 1823 until 1831 as a representative of Massachusetts.

After his death in 1851, this stone building was sold in 1852 to the newly formed Somerset Club, which used the property as its clubhouse until selling

Looking down Beacon Street. The Congregational House is in the distant center, and 8 and 10 Beacon, successively, are on the right, circa 1870. *Courtesy of Boston Athenaeum.*

it to the American Congregational Association in 1871. The Somerset Club then moved to the former David Sears estate at 42 Beacon Street, where it is still housed today.

The association then razed and remodeled the buildings, expanding in size and using this property as its headquarters until completion, in 1898, of their new building at 14 Beacon Street, at which time it sold the old Congregational House to the Houghton & Dutton Department Store.

The old building was then torn down, and in 1905 it was replaced by the expanding Houghton & Dutton Department Store, whose building now encompassed the entire block along the north side of Beacon Street from Tremont Street to Somerset Street.

4

SOMERSET STREET TO BOWDOIN STREET

North Side

9 BEACON

The architectural firm of Coolidge & Shattuck, which also designed the Boston Lying-In Hospital, designed this office building, erected in 1922. Known as the "Lawyer's Building," this structure initially housed over one hundred attorneys, primarily due to its proximity to the Suffolk County Courthouse. The ground floor had retail space and for many years in the late 1900s was occupied by Goodspeed's Bookshop, an antiquarian store specializing in books and maps.

The mansion house originally on this site was owned by Jerathmeel Bowers, who obtained it in 1786 through a recovered judgment against the estate of Joseph Sherburne Bowers, of Somerset, Massachusetts (hence Somerset Street). He willed the property to his son John, who laid out Somerset Street in 1803 to gain access to his lands north of Beacon Street. Bowers sold the property in 1803 to David Sears Sr., a respected merchant and philanthropic citizen who kept the large dwelling house where he had resided as a tenant since at least 1787. Sears's son and heir, the Honorable David Sears Jr., inherited the house in 1811 and lived there for thirty years until completing, in 1822, his new mansion house at 42 Beacon, now home of the Somerset Club.

In 1838, Sears replaced the house at the corner of Beacon and Somerset Streets with two "elegant and costly brick dwelling-houses"[18] that were to become 9–11 Beacon. The easterly house, 9 Beacon, was rented to various

Boston City Club, 11 and 9 Beacon, circa 1900. *Courtesy of Historic New England.*

tenants, with Abbot Lawrence residing here in 1840 and Frederick Tudor living here in 1851. (Tudor later lived at 34½ Beacon.) By the 1880s, the home was being used for business offices, and as early as 1907, it and 11 Beacon had become the home of the Boston City Club. Founded by Louis Brandeis, Edward Filene and others, by 1914 the club had a membership of over four thousand. Its popularity led to the construction of a new home at the corner of Somerset Street and Ashburton Place.

Numbers 9–11 Beacon were sold in 1916 to the Realty Investment Trust, which razed the existing buildings in 1922 and replaced them with the office building we see here today.

11 BEACON

This office building, 9 and 11 Beacon, was known as the "Lawyers Building," as it housed over one hundred attorneys. It replaced the double row houses built by David Sears in 1838.

This number was assigned to Sears's 1838 westerly double row house, which he rented to various tenants, including Samuel Lawrence in 1850, the first president of the Boston Board of Trade. Lawrence was influential, along with his brother Abbott, in founding the city of Lawrence, and together they owned cotton mills on the Merrimack River.

Numbers 11 and 9 Beacon, the "Lawyers Building," is at near right. The adjacent building is 15 Beacon.

In the late 1800s, this house was being used for business offices, and by 1908 it had been rented, along with 9 Beacon, by the newly formed Boston City Club. Sears's estate sold the houses in 1916 to the Realty Investment Trust, which razed them in 1922 and replaced them with the office building we see here today.

13 BEACON

This ten-story building, which today houses a luxury hotel named XV (Fifteen), was erected in 1903 by the Beacon Hill Trust on the site of 13 and 15 Beacon. It was designed by William Gibbons Preston, who also was architect of the Claflin Building at 20 Beacon Street and the Museum of Natural History on Berkeley Street.

The original house here, the Bromfield Mansion, was located on the north slope of the ridge that connected Cotton Hill and Beacon Hill[19] and was just to the west of the Sears land. The site was part of the estate of Edward

Bromfield, who had acquired it in 1742 from Samuel Sewall, the son of the Salem witchcraft trial judge of the same name.

Bromfield, a selectman of the town and a member of the general court, also served as an overseer of the poor for many years. His large home was described as follows:

> *It was of three stories, and richly furnished according to the fashion of the last* [eighteenth] *century...Three steep flights of stone steps ascended from Beacon Street to the front of the mansion; and behind it was a paved courtyard, above which rose successive terraces filled with flowers and fruit trees. On the summit, a summer house, elevated higher than the roofs of the houses which in 1861, form Ashburton Place, commanded a panoramic view of the harbor and environs...The hill on which this mansion stood— between those of Governor Bowdoin and David Sears both of subsequent erection—was leveled in 1845, and the site is now marked by Freeman Place Chapel and the adjoining houses on Beacon Street.*[20]

After Bromfield's death in 1756, the mansion house became the property, in 1763, of William Phillips, Bromfield's son-in-law. His daughter, Abigail, was married in the mansion house in 1769 to Josiah Quincy Jr., the revolutionary Patriot.[21]

His son, William Phillips Jr., was lieutenant governor of the state, and his grandson, Edward Bromfield Phillips, inherited the property in 1827. The

Edward Bromfield House, circa 1840.

house was rented out to boarders and was then razed in 1845. The property was divided in 1846 into lots, with two of them, 13 and 15 Beacon, fronting on Beacon Street. "In the rear was erected the Freeman Place Chapel with access from a way that still exists, although today widened, and in the front two fine dwelling houses were put up whose successive owners were among the first families of the city."[22] The lot, plus a brick house built by Jonathan Preston, was sold to George A. Whitney in 1848, and by 1858 it was a boardinghouse. It was later owned by C.H. Denny Co., wool importers, which converted its use to offices.

By 1902, the new owner, the Women's Club House Corporation, had razed the house, and the empty lot was sold to the Beacon Hill Trust the same year.

15 Beacon

This building, which today houses the luxury hotel XV (Fifteen), was erected in 1903 by the Beacon Hill Trust. The building originally housed the offices of the Boston Transit Commission on two floors and the Rapid Transit Commission, forerunner to today's MBTA. In 1920, the building was taken by eminent domain by the City of Boston from the Beacon Hill Trust "for school purposes." Beginning in 1923, it was occupied by the Boston School Committee.

The original house that was built here was sold by Edward Bromfield Phillips in 1847 to Samuel Cabot, who sold in 1848 to Seth A. Fowle, a well-known druggist.

Fowle retained the property until 1854, when it became the residence of Charles Homer of Homer and Sprague, merchants on India Wharf. The family lived in the house until 1896, when it was sold to the Beacon Hill Trust, and in 1903 the present building was erected.

Bowdoin Estate

17, 19, 21, 23, 25 and 27 Beacon

The estate of Governor James Bowdoin consisted of a three-story mansion house and lands fronting on Beacon Street as well as on Bowdoin Street (formerly Middlecott Street). Bowdoin had purchased the property in 1756 from his father-in-law, Captain John Erving, a Tory who had fled to England.

Bowdoin improved and remodeled the house, adding a brick barn. He also had one of the largest gardens in the city, full of varied fruit trees, including pears, peaches, apples and grapevines.

The house, as well as Edward Bromfield's adjoining house, was approached by a high flight of stone steps and set back from the street. It afforded the owners a view of the harbor similar to what could be seen from John Hancock's mansion.

During the Revolution, Bowdoin lived in the town of Middleborough, as the British general John Burgoyne occupied his house from 1775 until the British evacuation of Boston in 1776. Burgoyne was the general who later surrendered his forces, in 1777, to the Revolutionary army at Saratoga, New York, marking the turning point in the War for American Independence.

James Bowdoin II was a revolutionary Patriot and was elected president of the Massachusetts Council in 1776 after the evacuation of the city by the British. He presided over the reading of the Declaration of Independence from the balcony of the Old State House and supervised the removal of the British royal arms from the building, as witnessed by Abigail Adams, who reported, "Thus ends the royal authority in this state, and the people shall say Amen." In 1779, the General Court of Massachusetts requested that the towns elect representatives for a constitutional convention in an effort to create a new state constitution, and Bowdoin was selected as a delegate from Boston, along with John Adams from Braintree, the writer of the constitution. Bowdoin was elected by the representatives to be president of the convention and was subsequently chosen as chairman of the committee that drafted the constitution, which was adopted by the towns in 1780. Following this, an election was held for the first governorship of the commonwealth, with Bowdoin a candidate along with John Hancock. Hancock was elected, defeating Bowdoin by a considerable margin.

Bowdoin was subsequently elected governor in 1785 and was reelected in 1786, serving two one-year terms until 1787. His administration was marred by the occurrence of Shay's Rebellion, an armed insurrection by agrarian citizens as a consequence of onerous taxation and debt-collecting practices on the farmers in the western part of the state. He ran again for governor in 1788 and 1789 and was defeated soundly in both elections by the indomitable John Hancock.

Although Hancock retained the governorship, Bowdoin had the pleasure of accompanying the newly elected president, George Washington, to Sunday services at Bowdoin's church, the Brattle Street Church, upon Washington's 1789 visit to Boston during his tour of the states following his election. Washington also dined at Bowdoin's mansion with a large company, while he had only tea at Governor John Hancock's house. Bowdoin was an intimate friend of Benjamin Franklin's and was the first president and a founder of the American Academy of Arts and Science. He also was the first president of the First Bank of Boston founded in 1784.

Governor Bowdoin died in 1790, leaving, after the death of his wife, his Beacon Hill estate to his son, James Bowdoin III. James donated one thousand acres of land in Maine and $1,000 to found Bowdoin College, which was named for his father.

Upon James Bowdoin III's death, the estate passed to his heir and nephew, James Temple Bowdoin, who in 1836 razed the mansion house. In 1843, the property was divided into lots and was subsequently sold off in pieces. Six dwelling houses, 17, 19, 21, 23, 25 and 27 Beacon, were erected in a row on the north side of the street.

17 BEACON

This now empty lot was once part of the James Bowdoin estate that encompassed all the land west of the Bromfield estate to Bowdoin Street. The easternmost parcel became 17 Beacon and was sold in 1843 to W.F. Whitney, who was in the paint business. In 1868, he sold the house to Dio Lewis, who had as a tenant the Hotel Bellevue, which advertised Turkish baths in the basement and was "open at all hours."[23]

In 1894, the building was sold to the Boston Real Estate Trust, owner of the Hotel Bellevue. The new Hotel Bellevue building, erected in 1899, replaced the 19, 21 and 23 Beacon dwelling houses, but this house remained. Tax records show this as the "entrance of the Hotel Bellevue." In 1930, the building was replaced with a parking lot, which remains today.

19 BEACON

This address is presently assigned to the 21 Beacon Condominium Trust located at what was the Hotel Bellevue's first new building, erected in 1899. It replaced the houses at 19, 21 and 23 Beacon that had been built on the site of the James Bowdoin Estate.

This site was sold by the estate in 1843 to Abiel Chandler, who transferred the land in 1844 to Henry Holbrook, a dry goods merchant who built the house in

The Bellevue Hotel replaced Channing Hall.

1845. Holbrook defaulted on a mortgage, and in 1857 the property was transferred to Stephen Ball, physician. The Ball family retained ownership of the building and rented it to the Hotel Bellevue before 1880. In 1898, the family sold the hotel the property.

The hotel building, eleven stories in height, was luxurious and homelike and was both a standard hotel and a residential hotel catering to overnight, transient and long-term guests who used the hotel as apartments. Many notable Bostonians, including then senator John F. Kennedy, kept apartments there.[24] Peabody & Stearns, well-known architects, designed the hotel and also the Exchange Building and the Boston Post Building, as well as many residential shingle cottages, including the Vanderbilt estate, Elm Court, in Lenox.

Today, the Bellevue has been converted to condominiums and retains the same outward appearance as when it was erected one hundred years ago.

21 Beacon

This parcel of the Bowdoin estate was sold in 1843 to Robert C. Winthrop. In 1844, Jonathan Preston, mason, constructed a house on the lot, and it was sold in 1845 to Edward Brooks, lawyer. In 1854, Brooks sold the house to Robert C. Hooper, a merchant.

In 1887, Hooper sold to William Endicott Jr., who rented the property to the Hotel Bellevue as it expanded its size. In 1898, Endicott sold the building to the Bellevue Hotel, and in the same year 21 Beacon was razed, along with 19 and 23 Beacon, to be replaced with the new hotel building erected in 1899.

23 BEACON

The house originally located here was replaced in 1898 by the Hotel Bellevue building. The site was sold by the estate in 1843 to Gardner Brewer, a dry goods merchant who was head of Gardner, Brewer & Co.

In 1845, Brewer built a house on the land, where he remained until 1863, when he built a new mansion on the site of the John Hancock House.

Brewer, a successful businessman was also a philanthropist, and in 1868 he gave to the City of Boston a bronze fountain that is located on the Boston Common near the Park Street Mall. The fountain was cast in Paris and is a duplicate of a design by Lienard that received the gold medal at the Paris Exposition of 1855.[25]

Brewer's house was sold by his estate, and in 1868 it belonged to Hannah Rand, who retained ownership until 1876, when she sold to H.R. Endicott. Endicott used the property as an office building.

In 1885, the property was being rented by the Hotel Bellevue, and in 1898 it was sold, along with 21 Beacon, by William Endicott to the hotel. The house was razed in 1898, along with 19 and 21 Beacon, and was replaced by the new Hotel Bellevue building.

25 BEACON

The house originally here was constructed on a part of the Bowdoin estate division. In 1843, the estate sold the lot to Jonathan Preston, who then erected the house, which was sold in 1845 to Daniel Hammond.

The Hammond family retained ownership until 1884, when it was sold to the American Unitarian Association, which razed the original building and, in 1885, built a new structure designed by Peabody & Stearns as the headquarters for the association. It was named Channing Hall in honor of William Ellery Channing, a leading figure in the Universalist Church. Channing wrote many papers condemning slavery and was a strong abolitionist and supporter of William Lloyd Garrison's antislavery movement. He was minister of the Federal Street Church from 1803 until

Number 25 Beacon, Channing Hall, 1885, looking east toward Tremont Street. Named for William Ellery Channing, this was the headquarters for the American Unitarian Association. *Courtesy of the Bostonian Society/Old State House Museum.*

his death in 1842, and today there is a statue honoring him in the Boston Public Garden opposite the Arlington Street Church.

In 1925, the association purchased the William Endicott Jr. house at 32 Beacon Street, where it would erect its new headquarters and retain the address of 25 Beacon for the new site. At the same time, it sold 25 Beacon to the Hotel Bellevue, which proceeded to raze Channing Hall and in its place erect an addition to the existing hotel.

This new ten-story building was designed by architects Putnam and Cox and covered the sites of the original houses at 25 and 27 Beacon. It still exists today, converted into condominiums, with mostly the same outward appearance as when it was first built.

27 BEACON

The brick row house originally built here on part of the Bowdoin estate division was located at the northeast corner of Beacon and Bowdoin Streets. It was sold by the estate in 1843 to Theodore Chase, merchant. The Chase family retained ownership until Theodore's widow's death in 1884, when the heirs sold the property to the American Unitarian Association.

This house, along with 25 Beacon, was subsequently demolished and replaced in 1886 by Channing Hall, the new headquarters for the association. It was subsequently sold in 1925 to the Hotel Bellevue.

5

TREMONT STREET TO PARK STREET

South Side

TREMONT BUILDING

Standing in front of the King's Chapel and looking diagonally across Tremont Street (previously known as Common Street), where the Boston Common began, we would have seen, in the mid-1600s, the one-acre garden plot of Pastor John Wilson where now stands 73 Tremont Street, also known as the Tremont Building.

Reverend Wilson came to the New World as a minister with Governor John Winthrop and the Massachusetts Bay Company settlers. Arriving in Salem in 1630 but finding the town not to their liking, many of the settlers moved shortly thereafter to Charlestown. There, Wilson assisted in organizing a church in which he was ordained pastor. The church became the First Church of Boston.[26] Wilson stood for orthodoxy and conservatism and was one of the most rigid Puritans.

At the first meeting of the general court held in Charlestown in August 1630, it was determined that the public should provide houses for the ministers of the church. Charlestown, however, lacked a good source of drinking water, and this, along with poor living conditions, forced the group to look elsewhere for permanent settlement.

It was about this time that the group was invited to settle on the Shawmut Peninsula by Reverend William Blackstone, who since 1624 had been the lone inhabitant of what was to become the town of Boston. Boston had many springs and the benefit of a natural harbor that could easily accommodate future settlers. It was therefore in Boston, and not Charlestown, that Wilson's

The Tremont Building replaced the venerable Tremont House Hotel.

house was erected at what is now Devonshire Street, part of which was called Wilson's Lane.[27]

It was not long after the Common had been set aside for the settlement's use in 1634 that a one-acre section of garden plot was granted to Wilson for his services. Bounded on the south by the Granary Burial Ground,[28] it extended north and west up Beacon Street toward what is now Park Street at the Boston Common. To the north of Wilson's garden plot, where we now see One Beacon, was the property of future selectman of the town James Penn, who arrived with Winthrop in 1630.

Between these two properties, or through one of them, what was to become Beacon Street was first laid out in 1640. According to the Boston Town Records of March 30, 1640, "Also it is ordered that the streete from Mr. Atherton Haulghes to the Centry Hill to be layd out, so kept open forever." Mr. Haulghes resided at what is now the southwest corner of School and Washington Streets, which meant that the way along School Street from Washington Street to Tremont/Common Street and along Beacon Street toward Centry (Beacon) Hill was always to be kept open.

Wilson's garden plot land was sold in 1661 to Captain James Oliver, an officer of one of the military companies of Boston that was involved in the conflict called King Philip's War. These militia companies were the origin of the Ancient and Honorable Artillery Company that exists today.

By 1662, the property belonged to Zachariah Phillips, who divided it into lots, with the corner piece being sold to John Wilmott in 1662. Phillips was later killed in an ambush of the Boston militia in Brookfield during King Philip's War. The land stayed in the Wilmott family for over one hundred years until it was sold in 1764 to Daniel Hubbard. In 1825, Hubbard's estate sold to William H. Eliot, who was accumulating property on which to erect the Tremont House Hotel.

Other purchases, including the adjacent land of John Parker in 1827, gave Eliot ownership from the corner of Beacon and Tremont Streets to the bend in Beacon Street. He was then able to proceed fulfilling his master plan of building the Tremont House Hotel and laying out Tremont Place and its bordering houses.

William H. Eliot was the brother of Boston mayor Samuel A. Eliot and son of Samuel Eliot, who resided across the street at One Beacon. The Tremont House, America's first luxury hotel, whose cornerstone was laid on July 4, 1828, was designed by architect Isaiah Rogers. Rogers, who had worked in the office of Solomon Willard, architect of the Bunker Hill Monument, also designed the classical theater named the Howard Athenaeum, which would end its days as the famed Old Howard, a burlesque theater, destroyed by fire in the 1960s. Completed in 1829, the Tremont House was one of the first hotels with inside toilets and private baths and this, along with its corridor layout and large public rooms, made it "the father of the modern hotel."[29]

The hotel, which boasted 250 rooms with many arranged in suites, was host to many famous politicians, including Presidents Andrew Jackson, John Tyler and Andrew Johnson. Tyler was in Boston to attend the

Tremont House Hotel, 1890. Boston's first modern hotel. *Courtesy of the Bostonian Society/ Old State House Museum.*

dedication of the Bunker Hill Monument in 1843, when Daniel Webster gave one of his most memorable orations. Other guests included Charles Dickens, Henry Clay, Alexis de Tocqueville, John Wilkes Booth and William Makepeace Thackeray.

In 1858, another visitor, the future president of the Confederate States of America Jefferson T. Davis, was traveling south by ship with his family from Maine when a sudden illness affected his son and required immediate medical attention in Boston. The child was nursed back to health, and the family continued on its way, but not before Davis gave a speech at Faneuil Hall outlining why the Union should stay united even with the South retaining slavery as an institution.[30]

In 1832, following the death of William H. Eliot, the hotel was sold to the Tremont House proprietors, who retained ownership until 1859, when the property was sold to Joshua M. Sears. Sears owned the property until 1888, when he sold it to Frederick L. Ames.

The Tremont House ended its nearly three quarters of a century of service to the city when it was demolished in 1894, along with the houses on the east side of Tremont Place, and replaced, in 1896, with the eleven-story Tremont Building at 73 and 75 Tremont Street, which we see today. Designed by architects Winslow and Wetherell, who also designed the Jeweler's Building on Washington Street, it was an early elevator building, and although it had steel beams as floors, it still used solid masonry throughout, including the walls. Externally, this office building exists today much as it did when first erected.

TREMONT PLACE

The short roadway we see today between the Tremont Building and 6 Beacon Street is Tremont Place, which was laid out in 1829. Lined on either side with houses built by William H. Eliot, creator of the Tremont House Hotel, it gave access from Beacon Street to the Granary Burial Ground. The houses were numbered one through nine and eleven (there was no ten), with 1 and 2 Tremont Place having boundaries on Beacon Street (see map in "2 Beacon").

William Eliot originally rented these houses to various tenants, but he died not long after they were constructed, and his estate, administered by his brother, Samuel A. Eliot, was empowered to sell his real estate at auction for the payment of debts. The Tremont House Hotel was sold to a group of proprietors, and the individual houses bordering Tremont Place were auctioned off to the highest bidders as follows:

NUMBER 1 was located at the northwest corner of Tremont Place and Beacon Street and was alternately known as 6 Beacon Street. It was sold in 1833 to Nathan C. Keep, a surgeon dentist, and at about that time Nathan Hale, nephew of the revolutionary Patriot of the same name and father of the author and clergyman Edward Everett Hale, lived here. He was editor and publisher of the *Boston Daily Advertiser*, the first successful daily newspaper published in Boston.

The house was bought in 1846 by Elbridge G. Kelley, who kept the property until 1873, when it was sold along with 3 Beacon. In 1883, it was owned by Walter J. Otis, who sold it in 1891 to the Tremont Building Trust, which razed the houses—along with 5, 7, 9 and 11 Beacon—and replaced them with the existing office building.

NUMBER 2, which was located at the northeast corner of Tremont Place and Beacon Street, was sold in 1833 to Elisha Haskell, an auctioneer. In 1854, the owner was Paran Stevens, whose family retained ownership until 1895, when the estate sold it to the Tremont Building Trust, which subsequently razed the house and replaced it with the present Tremont Building.

6 BEACON

This early twentieth-century office building was erected on part of the original acre lot granted to Reverend John Wilson, pastor of the First Church. The property was sold in 1791 to Oliver Brewster, and in the 1798 U.S. Direct Tax list, Brewster is listed as having a "brick and wood dwelling" of three stories, a very sizable dwelling for the time.

In 1826, the site belonged to William H. Eliot, who had already purchased the property at the corner of Tremont and Beacon Streets and was to erect the Tremont House Hotel, as well as lay out Tremont Place.

In 1901, all the houses that he had built on the west side of Tremont Place, which encompassed virtually the same area as Oliver Brewster's estate, were razed and replaced by the eleven-floor office building designed by Goodwin and Siter of Tremont Street in Boston.

This edifice, named the Beacon Building, was one of the first to use all-steel framing along with brick and sandstone facing.[31] It was occupied initially by tenants predominantly in the legal and professional fields, mainly due to its proximity to the courthouses and government offices. This building's height was limited by the height restriction laws of 1891, and its exterior remains much the same as when it was originally constructed.

8 BEACON

This nine-story office building, formerly the addresses of 8 and 10, was erected on land that was part of the original acre lot granted to Reverend John Wilson and later sold to Captain James Oliver.

In 1798, the property, which included two houses, was owned by Elizabeth Loring and Mary Ruggles. In 1807, David Sears purchased it from them. In 1815, the selectmen's minutes state, "D. Sears being about to take down two wooden dwellings opposite his dwelling house on Beacon Street and to erect two brick houses on the lot."

Sears sold the property in 1823 to Amos Cotting and a group known as Fifty Associates,[32] of which Sears was a member. In 1824, 8 Beacon was maintained as a boardinghouse, with John Ewer, bookseller, living there. The second house, 10 Beacon, was used as a residential and retail business building and office space for physicians, lawyers and dentists.

Fifty Associates was a corporation set up in 1820: "Duty of directors to…make and agree for the purchase of buildings and estates as they may deem for the interest of the corporation to possess." In effect, it was an early real estate development firm with a percentage of its profits going to fund the Overseers of the Poor Charity. Between 1830 and 1865, this building had the address of 6 Beacon.

In 1899, 8 Beacon was replaced, along with 10 Beacon, by a nine-story office building—another example of an early steel frame construction using a granite base and brick walls above the second floor. It was designed by Andrew, Jacques and Rantoul, architects, who also did the east and west wing additions of the Massachusetts Statehouse.

The building has had minor alterations since construction and exists now much as it did at the end of the nineteenth century.

10 BEACON

This office building, now numbered 10 Beacon, replaced two 1825 Sears houses. The original western house was primarily used by business and professional people. From 1873 to 1883, future associate justice of the United States Supreme Court Oliver Wendell Holmes Jr. lived here with his new bride, Fanny Dixwell Holmes, in rooms above a drugstore located on the first floor.[33]

Between 1830 and 1845, when all Beacon Street addresses were given numbers, this building was assigned number eight. During that same period,

10 Beacon was assigned to the easternmost of four brick row house dwellings (10, 12, 14 and 16 Beacon) located on the adjacent property belonging to William Phillips.

These four dwellings were rented out; some were occupied by members of the Phillips family. In 1816, the brick dwelling at 10 Beacon was the home of the widow Ruth Emerson and her son, Ralph Waldo Emerson. Phillips sold the four houses in 1845 to the proprietors of the Boston Athenaeum, and the dwellings were subsequently razed in 1845 and 1846 to make way for the new home of the Boston Athenaeum.

10½ Beacon

This magnificent building is the home of the Boston Athenaeum, the oldest private library in the United States. Founded in 1807 in quarters on Congress Street and then housed on Pearl Street, the library moved here to its new home in 1849 in a new building situated on land that had originally been part of the Boston Common.

Numbers 8, 10 and 10½ Beacon (Boston Athenaeum). Numbers 8 (left) and 10 Beacon are modern buildings beyond the Athenaeum, 1902. *Courtesy of the Boston Athenaeum.*

Designed by architect Edward Clark Cabot, the building construction commenced in 1847 and was completed two years later. The property, which had included four brick row houses, was purchased by the proprietors of the Boston Athenaeum in 1845 from the Edward B. Phillips estate. Edward had inherited the property from his grandfather, William Phillips the elder, through his father, William Phillips Jr., a former lieutenant governor of Massachusetts. In 1795, William Phillips Jr. had purchased from the Town of Boston a piece of land that fronted on Beacon Street, adjacent to the almshouse, for the price of £910 (equal to $3,033.33 at that time). This land, plus the four brick house parcels, composed the Athenaeum lot. Edward Phillips, who died in 1848, left $100,000 to Harvard University for construction of an astronomical observatory and creation of the Phillips Professor of Astronomy.

Although this new Athenaeum building was considerably larger than the first one, by 1864 there was need for additional space, as the Fine Arts Department needed "a new and permanent home where there would be room for expansion."[34] Fortunately, an adjacent building at 11 Tremont Place had been purchased, and the proprietors had Cabot design a new facility to house the painting and sculpture collections. This plan was never implemented, however, for even though the Athenaeum also purchased 7 and 9 Tremont Place, the three buildings were used only as rental properties.

The eventual sale of these properties on Tremont Place was to help finance the library's potential move to a new facility at the corner of Arlington and Newbury Streets across from the Public Garden.[35] This planned move was the result of the recent erection, on the corner of Beacon and Tremont Streets, of the nearby so-called tall skyscraper building. Its size interfered with the natural light and air that the Athenaeum deemed essential to its members' enjoyment of the premises and posed a potential fire hazard from falling walls in case of fire in the surrounding skyscrapers. Because of these facts, the decision was made by the library trustees to sell the Tremont Place buildings, in 1901, to the Tremont Building Trust.

This move to the Public Garden site never occurred, however, due to considerable dissension among the members, who did not want to abandon the existing building. The decision to remain at this location led to the inevitable refurbishing of the structure, and in 1913–14 the Athenaeum was completely renovated, fireproofed and enlarged when the fourth and fifth floors were added.

The interior itself was modified a number of times, including the latest renovations that started in 1999 and were completed in 2002. These latest changes began by emptying the premises of its treasures and transferring them to various storage facilities and to locations that permitted access to most of the book facilities. The building reopened in September 2002 and is now fully air-conditioned and climate controlled, allowing the proper temperature and humidity levels to maintain the collection into the foreseeable future.

The inclusion of a half as part of the address originated from the insertion of new buildings between successively numbered addresses. Hence, when the Boston Athenaeum was constructed, it was placed between 10 and 12 Beacon—11 Beacon was on the north side of the street—and to preclude the need for renumbering the entire street, the address of 10½ Beacon was added.

12 BEACON

This building, also numbered 14 Beacon, was erected in 1898 and became the new headquarters for the American Congregational Society after it moved here from its former offices, which it had outgrown, at the Congregational House on the corner of Beacon and Somerset Streets.

The building was designed by architects Shepley, Rutan & Coolidge, whose other Boston structures include the Ames Building and South Station. They also designed the summer home, Hildene, of Robert Todd Lincoln, which today is a house museum located in Manchester, Vermont.

This site, originally part of the Common in 1660, was part of "that parcel of land occupied for an almshouse and workhouse, and other purposes" owned by the Town of Boston. After deciding to construct a new almshouse elsewhere, the town sold this property at public auction in 1801 as lot number six, which was to become 12 and 14 Beacon, to Thomas Amory.

Amory sold the land in 1807 to sisters Mary and Sarah Payne with the provision that space be made (when building a house) for the ventilation of his wine storage vaults that extended under Beacon Street. The vaults had been built under Amory's house, the adjacent property, which he had recently sold to Samuel Dexter. The Payne sisters proceeded to build a double house on the land with a central arch that led to the entrances to the two residences. This archway extended from Beacon Street to the open area in the back that bordered on the Granary Burial Ground. The ownership continued to the nephew of the sisters, William Payne, one of the first insurance underwriters in the city.

The house was sold by William Payne's estate to Frances Hicks Rollins in 1844 (14 Beacon was sold to James K. Mills on the same date). In 1866, Eben

Left: Number 14 Beacon, the American Congregational Building, 1898.

Below: Numbers 12 (left) and 14 Beacon, the Payne sisters' house, at right foreground with the Athenaeum beyond, 1890. The double house was replaced by the American Congregational Building. *Courtesy of the Bostonian Society/Old State House Museum.*

W. Rollins of Bagley, Rollins & Co., commission merchants, sold to Charles Merriam, a railroad magnate, who proceeded to remodel the house. In 1874, Merriam sold to Charles O. Whitmore, who already owned 14 Beacon.

Whitmore sold the house to the Lexington Building Association in 1875 (along with 14 Beacon), which rented to various tenants, including the City of Boston, for offices. In 1896, it sold both houses to the American Congregational Association, which constructed its new headquarters.

14 BEACON

This building was erected in 1898 as the headquarters for the American Congregational Society. The original house had been sold in 1844 by descendants of the Payne sisters' nephew William Payne to James K. Mills on the same date as the sale of 12 Beacon.

Mills retained the house until 1858, when he sold to Charles O. Whitmore, commission merchant and owner of the firm Charles O. Whitmore and Son. In 1866, Whitmore was noted in the city records as "remodeling the store front of the building." In 1875, Whitmore transferred the house to the Lexington Building Association, which rented out the building until selling it to the American Congregational Association in 1896.

16 BEACON

This four-story building is unusual as it is the only example of residential architecture from the early nineteenth century remaining in this section of Beacon Street. Now home to the Boston Bar Association, it has been altered many times over its nearly two-hundred-year existence yet still retains the appearance of a period residence.

The land on which the house sits was a section of lot five of the almshouse, which the Town of Boston sold to Thomas Amory in 1801. Amory subsequently sold the same land to Samuel Dexter in 1807, along with Amory's other properties along Beacon Street. At about the same time, the adjacent building to the west, 20 Beacon (an ell of the Amory House), was separated into two properties, with the entrance to the rear section, 18 Beacon, adjacent to 16 Beacon's entryway.

Robert Fletcher, builder of 16 Beacon, purchased the property in 1809 from Dexter, and in 1827 it belonged to Chester Harding. Harding was an

Numbers 16 (left), 18 and 20 Beacon. The "Boston University College of Liberal Arts" sign is on 18 Beacon. The "Offices of the College" sign is on 20 Beacon. *Courtesy of the Boston Athenaeum.*

American portrait painter of famous personages, including Daniel Boone and the first United States Supreme Court chief justice, John Marshall, whose painting is exhibited at the nearby Boston Athenaeum. Harding lived here for only three years and subsequently rented a house at 5 Tremont Place.

In 1863, the owner was Levi Bartlett, a Boston merchant who bequeathed the house to his daughter Martha, wife of Dr. Henry Clay Angell, professor of ophthalmology at Boston University and the author of many papers on diseases of the eye. Angell also wrote on literary and art subjects and was president of the Boston Philharmonic Society. Martha Angell was an avid art collector, having acquired works of Corot, Monet, Turner and others, many of which she gave to the Museum of Fine Arts.

The Angells lived there for almost fifty years, and in her will in 1919, Martha Angell left the estate to the Unitarian Association. In 1919, the association renovated and adapted the house for use as an annex until 1962, when the property was sold to the Boston Bar Association for use as its headquarters, which continues today.

18 BEACON

The Claflin Building, now 18 and 20 Beacon, today remains similar in appearance to when it was initially erected. Originally the home of Boston University, it was designed by architect William G. Preston and named for Lee

Claflin, one of the founders of Boston University and the father of William Claflin, governor of Massachusetts from 1869 to 1871.

It was built on part of the almshouse site and, as lot number five, was sold in 1801 by the Town of Boston to Thomas Amory, who erected, in 1804, the original building at 20 Beacon as an adjunct to his main residence. This became a separate dwelling when in 1806, Amory sold a portion of his estate to Dr. John Jeffries.

Jeffries was the surgeon general of the British forces in Boston prior to their evacuation in 1776 and had identified the body of General Joseph Warren amongst the dead at Bunker Hill. Jeffries left the city with the Loyalists, accompanying

The Claflin Building replaced 18 and 20 Beacon and was named for William Claflin, one of the founders of Boston University.

them to Halifax and from there to London. He was also an adventurer, as he accompanied the French aeronaut Francois Blanchard on the first balloon crossing of the English Channel in 1785.

Jeffries was allowed to return to Boston in 1790, as he was from an old and respected family, and because of a shortage of physicians, he was able to set up a medical practice that became successful and eventually included his son of the same name.

Jeffries sold the property in 1807 to William Payne, and by 1819 this rear building was owned by Andrew Ritchie, a son-in-law of Harrison Gray Otis. Ritchie sold in 1835 to Benjamin Guild, whose estate sold in 1860 to Mary and Henry G. Clark, physician. In 1873, this property and the front half of this house (20 Beacon), which Clark had purchased in 1868, were transferred to the newly established Boston University.

Boston University had been founded in 1869, and its College of Liberal Arts, organized in 1873, immediately occupied the building. The original houses (18 and 20 Beacon) were replaced in 1884 by the six-story brownstone building that exists today and is presently commercial condominiums.

20 BEACON

This six-story brownstone building, numbered 18 and 20 Beacon, was erected in 1884 and was known as the Claflin Building, as it was named for Lee Claflin, one of the founders of Boston University.

The front half of the house was separated from the rear portion, whose entrance was through an arched passageway on the westerly side of 16 Beacon. Amory sold this front section to Samuel Dexter in 1807.

Dexter's widow, Catherine, sold this property in 1835 to John Heard, who sold in 1854 to Matthias Sawyer of Portland, Maine. Sawyer was already the owner of the main Amory House. He was unmarried but had an adopted daughter, Lydia N. Osgood of Newburyport, to whom he devised his property on Beacon Street. She had married Curtis B. Raymond in 1849, and the Amory House is still remembered by some as the Raymond Building.

By 1868, the house belonged to Henry G. Clark, physician, who had been inspector in chief of army hospitals during the Civil War. He had purchased 18 Beacon in 1860, thus unifying both sections of this ell of the original Amory House under the same ownership for the first time in over sixty years. In 1873, the building was owned by Boston University.

AMORY TICKNOR HOUSE

22 Beacon

At the southeast corner of Beacon and Park (formerly Sentry or Centry) Streets stands the much changed but still impressive Amory Ticknor House. Erected in 1804, this structure is one of the two oldest existing houses on Beacon Street (the other is the Phillips-Winthrop House).

The site was originally part of the Common and had been set aside by the Town of Boston in 1660 for space to build an almshouse to be used as a home for the poor, aged or infirm. The first almshouse building was wood and was erected in 1662 (and rebuilt as a two-story brick building in

Amory-Ticknor House, erected in 1804 on the site of the almshouse.

1686 after a fire) with the assistance of donations from townspeople and £120 from Captain Robert Keayne, the founder of the Military Company of the Massachusetts, afterward known as the Ancient and Honorable Artillery Company.

The almshouse covered an area that fronted 66 feet on Sentry (Park) Street and 150 feet on Beacon Street. Adjacent to and south of it on Sentry Street were located the adjoining buildings housing the bridewell and workhouse. The bridewell was used for housing disorderly and insane persons, and the workhouse, which was built in 1738, housed the vagrants and dissolute of the town. In 1795, the town decided that these facilities were no longer able to provide the housing necessary for its unfortunate and criminal citizenship and voted to build new facilities on the northwest side of Beacon Hill on Leverett Street. Designed by Charles Bulfinch, this new structure was completed and occupied by the end of 1800. The Beacon Street properties were then divided into six lots, and the buildings and lands were sold at auction.

The southeast corner lot of Beacon and Park Streets was sold at auction in 1801 by the town to Thomas Amory, a successful Boston merchant and the highest bidder, at $8,200.

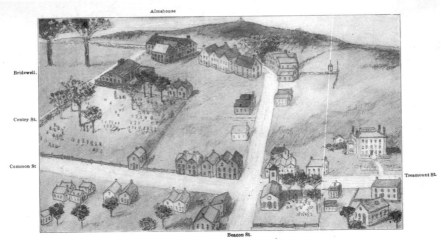

PARK, BEACON, AND TREMONT STREETS IN 1722

Conjectural Bonner map of 1722, showing the location of the almshouse.

In 1804, Amory proceeded to build a house designed by architect Charles Bulfinch, who had recently completed the new Massachusetts Statehouse located almost directly across from Amory's property.

This Bulfinch-designed mansion house was immediately known as "Amory's Folly" due to its immense size and pretentiousness in the Georgian style. While constructing this house, of which 18 and 20 Beacon were a part, he received permission from the town to build a range of wine and coal vaults under Beacon Street that were to be part of his house, connected to the main house by a series of arches. These vaults and arches still exist today, extending approximately twenty feet from the foundation wall north under Beacon Street,[36] and until recently, the entrance to them could still be seen in the basement floor of the premises.

Unfortunately, shortly after the completion of the houses, Amory went bankrupt, due in part to the high cost of this structure, and was notified of his financial ruin just as he was welcoming guests into his new home at a housewarming.

After his financial reversals, Amory proceeded to divide the estate into two sections by partitioning the house into a northern and southern section. In 1806, he sold the southern section, which included a section of the house, now 9 Park Street, and land, to Dr. John Jeffries for $40,000. This property extended one hundred feet along Park Street, starting from a partition wall erected by Amory (a vague outline of which can be seen today) and running parallel with the side of the mansion house on Beacon Street and southerly from the center of the partition wall origin on the Park Street side to the land of John Gore.

Amory-Ticknor House, circa 1885, showing much of the original Bulfinch design.

The northern section of the property, which included part of the Amory House and the land where 16 Beacon was built, was bounded by Beacon and Park Streets. Amory first rented the corner house to a Mrs. Carter for use as a boardinghouse and then sold the entire section to Samuel Dexter in 1807.

Dexter was an accomplished attorney who was both a United States congressman (1793–95) and United States senator (1799–1800). Under the administration of John Adams, he was appointed secretary of war and then, in 1801, secretary of the treasury, continuing in that cabinet post under President Jefferson. He is also noted for his appearance before the United States Supreme Court, representing the merchants of Boston who were arguing against the Embargo Act of 1807, which was ruining them and which they claimed was unconstitutional. Although he lost the case, he was made famous by his presentation and arguments.

Dexter died in 1816,[37] and his widow, Katherine, retained ownership of the house until 1831, when she sold it to Richard Cobb while retaining 20 Beacon and renting the same. In 1824, 22 Beacon was occupied by a club that housed the Marquis de Lafayette, who visited Boston during a tour of the United States.

Cobb sold in 1836 to Matthias Sawyer. Sawyer left the property in his will of 1857 to his adopted daughter, Lydia N. Osgood, who married Curtis B. Raymond.

The southern section of the property was retained by Dr. Jeffries for only one year. Jeffries sold it in 1807 to William Payne, who divided the property into sections and, in 1809, sold the mansion house section on Centry Street, now 9 Park Street, to his brother-in-law,[38] Christopher Gore. He sold the balance of the land south of the Amory House along Park Street to Christopher's nephew, John Gore, who eventually built 7 and 8 Park Street.

In 1813, Christopher Gore, governor of Massachusetts in 1809, was chosen United States senator from Massachusetts (1813–16). He was the builder of Gore Place in Waltham and endower of Gore Hall at Harvard University. He sold 9 Park Street, in 1816, to Andrew Ritchie, who lived in the house even after selling the property to his father-in-law, Harrison Gray Otis, in 1824. Otis sold to George Ticknor in 1830, hence the derivation of the name Amory-Ticknor House.

George Ticknor, author of the *History of Spanish Literature*, had a large and extensive library that was a social center, with frequent visitors such as Daniel Webster, William Prescott and Edward Everett. In the 1850s, he was estimated to have had the second-largest library in Boston (the largest was that of Charles Francis Adams), with some thirteen thousand volumes consisting of classics, modern literature and, particularly, Spanish and Portuguese literature. Ticknor was one of the founders of the Boston Public Library, and part of his sizable collection was bequeathed to the library upon his death.

Ticknor's wife, Anna Eliot Ticknor, sister of Boston mayor Samuel Eliot, was regarded as "the social queen" of Boston,[39] and following her death in 1884 the estate was transferred to George's daughter, Elsie Dexter, who had married a relative of Samuel Dexter.[40] In 1908, 9 Park Street was owned by Rose Dexter and was being rented to the Society of Arts and Crafts. In 1931, it was owned by the 9 Park Street Trust, which owned it as late as 1940. Today this house is condominiums.

24 BEACON

This address is presently assigned to the Massachusetts Statehouse.

26 BEACON

This was the prior address for 20 Beacon between 1830 and 1866.

6

Bowdoin Street to Joy Street

The Boston Common

The Boston Common is perhaps the best-known public park in the United States and is the pride of the city's residents. It was created from land granted to the town of Boston's first settler, William Blackstone, and has existed with slight alterations to its form for nearly four hundred years.

In 1634, Blackstone sold his interest in the Shawmut Peninsula to the Town of Boston, along with forty-four of the fifty acres that had been allocated to him by the selectmen in 1633. The six acres he retained for himself contained his house and gardens, while the forty-four acres he sold to the Town of Boston were to become the Boston Common. In the town records of March 30, 1640, it is written:

> *Also agreed upon that henceforth there shal be no land granted either for house plott or garden to any person out of the open ground or Common field which is left between the Centry Hill and Mr. Colbrons end; except 3 or 4 lotts to make up the street from bro. Robth Walkers to the Round Marsh*

This order preserved this common space for the common good of the inhabitants.

The name of Common Street, now Tremont Street, indicates the easternmost boundary of the early Common. Some of its area was used for various public purposes, such as the Granary Burial Ground, so named because of its proximity to the Granary, which was at the corner of Park and Tremont Streets and was replaced by the Park Street Church.

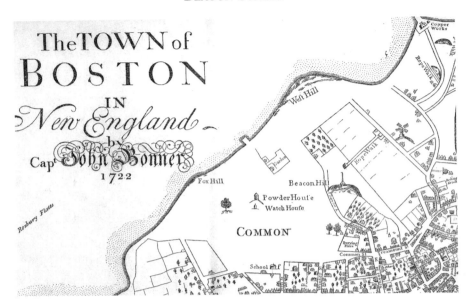

Bonner map of 1722, showing the Boston Common, the Beacon upon Beacon Hill and Bannister's Gardens, originally Blackstone's Gardens.

View from the Boston Common, 1804. Engraving by Ritchie. At right is the Amory Ticknor House, and at the extreme left is the Phillips-Winthrop House with its entrance on Beacon Street.

Other early public buildings, including the almshouse (replaced by the Amory-Ticknor House), the bridewell and workhouse, also were erected on that section of the Common.

The original Common land along Beacon Street, where today we find the Tremont Building and the Boston Athenaeum, had been granted to the First Church pastor, John Wilson, for his garden. The property was eventually sold to various owners and never returned to being part of the Common.

The western boundary of the Common was the shore of the Charles River Basin, where in the late 1700s ropewalks were erected. When Charles Street was laid out, the ropewalks disappeared, and Charles Street itself became the permanent boundary of the Common.

To the south, Boylston Street was the boundary, and to the north, Beacon Street. These remain the boundaries today.

SHAW MEMORIAL

This memorial, designed by Augustus Saint Gaudens and McKim, Mead and White and dedicated in 1897 to the memory of Robert Gould Shaw and his regiment, is located opposite the entrance to the Massachusetts Statehouse. Shaw was colonel of the Fifty-fourth Massachusetts Infantry,

Shaw Memorial, designed by Augustus St. Gaudens and dedicated to Robert Gould Shaw and the first all-black regiment sent to fight in the Civil War.

the first regiment of free African American men to fight in the Civil War. In 1863, Shaw and 40 percent of his men were killed in an attack on Fort Wagner in Charleston Harbor, South Carolina.

DANIEL D. DENNISON ROGERS ESTATE

Just to the west of Bowdoin Street, where today we find the east wing extension of the Massachusetts Statehouse, once existed the estate of Daniel Dennison Rogers, which was bordered by Bowdoin, Beacon and Mt. Vernon Streets. Until the statehouse east wing was constructed, Mt. Vernon Street, also known as Sumner Street, continued from its present location easterly past the statehouse and then turned southerly where the General Hooker statue stands, ending at Beacon Street.

D.D. Rogers, a dry goods merchant who also dealt in real estate, stocks and notes, had the property conveyed to him in 1782 by the Commonwealth of Massachusetts. Following the American Revolution, Massachusetts had confiscated the estate from Charles Ward Apthorp, a Loyalist. Apthorp, a brother-in-law to Charles Bulfinch, had been a business partner of William Molineaux, one of the distinguished Patriots of the town who had built a mansion house on the property he had acquired in 1760 from John Alford.

Daniel Dennison Rogers House, circa 1830, now part of the east statehouse grounds. *Courtesy of the Boston Athenaeum.*

Molineaux, an actor in the Boston Tea Party, was an influential member of the Sons of Liberty, the most fanatical group advocating independence from Britain, and was on the committee that demanded of Governor Hutchinson the removal of the British troops after the Boston Massacre in 1770.[41] Apthorp had extended funds to him during the hard times of the British closure of the Port of Boston, and following Molineaux's death in 1774, his entire estate passed on to Apthorp. His ownership did not last long, however. When the Revolution broke out, the entire estate was confiscated, and Apthorp lost everything he possessed.[42]

Upon acquiring the property, Rogers removed Molineaux's house and built a new three-story mansion house, also obtaining additional land to the east through which he ran a private way connecting Middlecott Street to Beacon. This Middlecott Street was finally connected from Cambridge Street to Beacon Street and was renamed Bowdoin Street to honor the former governor and Patriot whose estate was just to the east. Rogers then sold off lots along Bowdoin Street, with one piece of property being sold to William Thurston in 1802. Thurston subsequently built a house there that suffered an unusual fate. Thurston's land and the story of his house was described in one of Bowditch's Gleaner articles:

> *This land adjoined the extreme summit of Beacon Hill. His west line was on the lot 6 rods square, in the centre of which stood the beacon or monument itself...Mr. Thurston, in 1804, erected on his estate a house, from which he could literally look down upon all his fellow-citizens. It stood in about the centre of his land from north to south, while it was but two feet distant on the west from the monument lot. It was approachable only by steps, and it was even found necessary to hoist up all his wood, etc. In...a very celebrated law case—of Thurston vs. Hancock— from which it appears that the defendants in 1811 dug down their land on the west 60 feet below the original level and the earth fell in, leaving bare his cellar wall, etc., and rendering his house unsafe, so that it had to be taken down.*

In 1811, the Town of Boston sold to a group that included John Hancock, nephew of the famous Patriot of the same name, and Samuel Spear the six square rods of land on which the famous beacon of Beacon Hill had stood since 1635. The beacon had been replaced in 1790 by a column designed by Charles Bulfinch as a monument to the Revolutionary War and had at its base four tablets describing important events of the Revolution. The new owners, after dismantling the Bulfinch monument, proceeded to "dig down" the hill in order to sell the valuable gravel of which it was composed. The

William Thurston House, circa 1811, showing Beacon Hill excavation. *Courtesy of the Boston Athenaeum.*

inscribed tablets on the original monument were saved in a basement of the statehouse and later reinstalled on the monument that exists today on the east side of the 1895 Charles E. Brigham addition.

Thurston's damages were laid at $20,000, and the house was subsequently moved to One Beacon Hill Place. The court decision was that "no action lay for the owner of the house for damage done to the house; but that *he was entitled to an action for damage arising from the falling of his natural soil into the pit so dug.*" It was founded on the idea that Mr. Thurston must have known that his next neighbors "had a right to build equally near to the line, or to dig down the soil for any other lawful purpose" and that "from the shape and nature of the ground, it was impossible to dig there without causing excavations."

This opinion has always been unsatisfactory to many of the profession. The town had owned these ninety-nine square feet on the summit of the hill, with the thirty-foot way to them, for the purpose of sustaining a beacon and as a spot accessible to all citizens and strangers. It could not reasonably have been supposed that "for any sum of money, much less that for *a mere mess of pottage*, the town could have been induced to part with the one object that made it indisputably the queen of all the cities on this continent."[43]

Following the death of Rogers and his wife, in 1833 the estate was sold at auction by the heirs, who divided the property into six lots upon which were eventually built dwelling houses. One parcel, bordering Beacon Street, Bowdoin Street and Mt. Vernon Street, was sold by the estate in 1833 to Cornelius Coolidge, architect, who designed and built at least one house on the divided lot, with the westerly site having the address of One Mt. Vernon Street.

In 1894, the Commonwealth of Massachusetts proceeded to take the property of the then current owners, Moses Williams and Edmund Quincy, thus expanding the statehouse grounds eastward in expectation of a substantial enlargement to the statehouse that occurred in 1914.

The buildings on these sites were razed, and the extension of Mt. Vernon Street, where now the statue of Civil War general Joseph Hooker stands, was erased and absorbed into the east side of the grounds. A statue of Quaker Mary Dyer, who was hanged on the Boston Common in 1660, also stands in front of the east wing.

The appropriation of these buildings preceded similar takings by the commonwealth of properties along Beacon Street on the west side of the statehouse grounds by some twenty years.

MASSACHUSETTS STATEHOUSE

Situated close to the top of Beacon Hill is the new Massachusetts Statehouse. This Charles Bulfinch–designed masterpiece, dedicated in 1798, replaced the Old State House building on State Street that was once the seat of the British colonial government.

When the American Revolution had been won, an early goal of the Patriots was a new seat of government, and although other cities such as Worcester and Fall River vied for the site of the capital, Boston was chosen without much dissension. This location was situated just under the peak of the famous Beacon Hill and oversaw the growing city in all directions, including seaward, from where its commercial success emanated.

The lot of land upon which the new statehouse was to be erected was known as "Governor Hancock's pasture"; it was part of the estate that was purchased from the heirs of Governor Hancock by the citizens of the town of Boston in 1795 and transferred from the town to the Commonwealth of Massachusetts that same year.

Left: Massachusetts Statehouse, designed by Charles Bulfinch in 1795, in its present configuration with the west wing addition.

Below: John Hancock estate plan of 1795, including the pasture where the statehouse stands today.

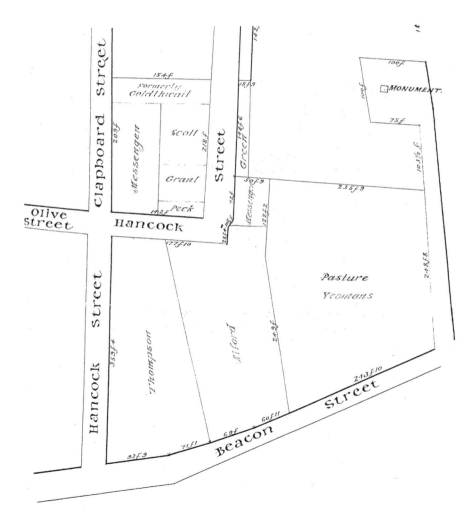

It is interesting to note that Governor Hancock, when nearing death in 1793, had instructed his attorney to change his will, leaving this "pasture lot" to the citizens of Boston, but he passed on before he was able to implement his wishes. Such was the intended largesse of one of Boston's most, if not the most, patriotic and generous citizens.

The new Massachusetts Statehouse was designed by renowned American architect Charles Bulfinch, designer of the Amory House at 22 Beacon and the Harrison Gray Otis House at 44 Beacon. Bulfinch also worked on the design and completed construction of the United States Capitol Building in Washington, D.C. The cornerstone of the new statehouse was laid on July 4, 1795, by Revolutionary War heroes Paul Revere and Samuel Adams and was brought to the site by fifteen white horses representing the number of states in the Union at that time. The building was completed three years later and was officially opened when the Massachusetts legislature met for the last time on January 11, 1798, in the Old State House and then proceeded—in a ceremonial parade that included Bulfinch in a prominent position—from that building up Beacon Hill to the new statehouse. This ceremony was reenacted on January 11, 1998, in celebration of the bicentennial of the dedication of the statehouse and was presided over by Governor Paul Cellucci and distinguished state officials.

An 1800 engraving by A. Bowen of the "New State House" with the Hancock House and stables.

Considered by many to be the most beautiful building in Boston, it has long been cherished by many of its native sons and daughters. Poet and author Oliver Wendell Holmes, although born in Cambridge, lived almost his entire life in Boston, and it is here where he wrote, in the memorable *The Autocrat of the Breakfast Table*, that the "Boston State House is the hub of the solar system."[44]

The building did not keep its pure Bulfinch design for long. It was modified first in 1831 with an addition designed by Isaiah Rogers, architect of the Tremont House, to house records and papers of the commonwealth in fireproof rooms.

A second addition, designed by Gridley F. Bryant and built between 1853 and 1856, was a four-story wing in the rear of the original structure. A third addition, of yellow brick and also in the rear, was completed in 1895 and designed by Charles E. Brigham, but it necessitated the removal of the first two additions. The final change was added between 1914 and 1917 and consisted of two wings designed by the firm of Andrews, Sturgis and Chapman. These wings added to the original structure on the east and west sides were constructed of white Vermont marble and granite and represent the present configuration.

The reverence that the residents of Boston and Massachusetts held for the Bulfinch statehouse was exhibited when a furor arose over the construction of the high-rise building called the Tudor, erected in 1887 at the western corner of Joy and Beacon Streets. This building's height prevented some Beacon Hill and Back Bay residents from a view of the golden dome (covered in gold leaf since 1874), and concerned city and state officials were determined to take legislative action to prevent further impediments to a clear view.

The result was a law passed in 1891 limiting building height in the cities of Massachusetts to 125 feet, or about eleven stories. Subsequent legislation in 1902 restricted building heights in Boston to 70 feet and, finally, 80 feet in the residential area to the west of the statehouse. In 1901, a height restriction of 100 feet for buildings facing the recently expanded statehouse grounds to the east of the Bulfinch façade was voted into law for protection from the east, as demonstrated by the expansion of the Hotel Bellevue,[45] ensuring that views of the golden dome would not be encroached upon again.

There was equal protection needed for the views *from* the statehouse, as explained in a dramatic description of the view from the cupola atop the dome written in 1838 in E.C. Wine's *A Trip to Boston*:

I have stood upon the keep of Carisbrooke Castle in the Isle of Wight, on the Leaning Tower of Pisa; on the dome of the Cathedral at Florence; on the summits of Gibraltar, Vesuvius, the Acro-Corinthus at Corinth, Greece; the Acropolis of Sardis in Asia Minor; and on many other elevated points in all the four continents. And I declare that few of the prospects thus obtained are equal, and fewer still superior, to that enjoyed from the State House at Boston.[46]

Expansion of the grounds and building to the east caused the taking of the extension of Mt. Vernon Street, which connected to Beacon Street, while the west wing displaced 28, 29, 30 and 31 Beacon on the site of the Hancock mansion and stables.

The Massachusetts Statehouse remains the center of historical Boston.

28 (29) BEACON

After 1866, this was the address of the John W. Trull House, previously 29 Beacon. The house was built on land that was part of the John Hancock estate to the east of his mansion house and was partitioned off in 1819 to Samuel Spear, who had successively married two of the daughters of Hancock's sister, Mary (Hancock) Perkins.[47] Spear mortgaged the property with Israel Thorndike, the ubiquitous developer, the same year, and upon Spear's death, the undeveloped property was transferred to Thorndike probably as payment for his mortgage.

In 1824, the land was sold to John Hubbard, Henry Hubbard and Cornelius Coolidge, who in 1826 divided the property into seven lots running along what was a continuation of Hancock Street through to Beacon Street. One lot facing Beacon Street was sold in 1829 to John W. Trull, a well-known liquor distiller who was also president of the North Bank.

Trull's estate sold the house in 1901 to Franklin H. Beebe, who owned the property until 1918, when it was taken by the Commonwealth of Massachusetts for use as open space in front of the statehouse's west wing extension.

John Hancock House Estate

In front of the west wing of the Massachusetts Statehouse on the granite wall that borders Beacon Street there is a plaque indicating the site where the home of Governor John Hancock once stood:

Here stood the residence of
John Hancock
a prominent and patriotic
merchant of Boston, the first
signer of the Declaration of
American Independence and
first governor of Massachusetts
under the state constitution

Erected 1737   Removed 1863

John Hancock inherited his house, tragically demolished in 1863, through his aunt Lydia Hancock's dower rights from her husband, Thomas Hancock, original builder of the mansion house. Thomas Hancock had purchased sections of land from John Alford and various other sellers between 1735 and 1759; these together consisted of all the land fronting Beacon Street between the Mt. Vernon Street extension and Joy Street.

Thomas Hancock was a successful merchant, bookseller, publisher and manufacturer of paper. His marriage to his business associate Daniel Henchman's

John Hancock House, circa 1860, a few years before its tragic demolition.

daughter, Lydia, also provided him with a substantial dowry, which he used to expand his investments and property holdings. After establishing himself as a successful businessman, he decided to build a house representative of his new social position and chose the sparsely populated southern slope of Beacon Hill as an area where he could have a sizable estate at a reasonable price.

While the architect is not recorded, it is possible that John James, an English architect who worked under Christopher Wren, was a collaborator, as "the most likely period for his visit to Boston was in 1736 when it is not improbable that he was consulted by Thomas Hancock as to the architecture of the house to be erected."[48]

"The house was of stone, built in the substantial manner favored by the wealthier Bostonians. The walls were massive. A balcony projected over the entrance-door upon which opened a large window of the second story"[49] (from which one could see Boston Harbor and the Blue Hills in Milton).

John Hancock was seven years of age when his father died, and his uncle Thomas adopted him and brought him from Braintree to Boston and to his amazing Beacon Hill mansion. While still a youth, John's uncle sent him to England to be educated in the European ways and to learn business on that side of the Atlantic. While there, he had attended the funeral of King George II and witnessed the excitement leading up to the coronation of George III, who was later to put a price on his head for his activities.

John returned to America in late 1761 and soon after was brought into his uncle's business as a partner. As Thomas's health declined, John, at the age of twenty-six, became the operating manager of the business and was able to become fully capable of running the company by 1763. Upon the death of his uncle in 1764 and his wife, who died in 1777, John inherited his uncle's immense fortune, including various lands and the Beacon Street estate.

During the 1760s, John Hancock had become involved in the revolutionary movement and became friends with Samuel Adams and his cousin and future president John Adams. Hancock was an unusual Patriot, as he used his wealth as well as his zeal to support the Revolution against the British.

Following the start of the rebellion in April 1775, Hancock became a wanted man who went into hiding while leaving his house in Boston to the British forces. During this time, his home was occupied by the British for use by their generals, including General Henry Clinton, who became the supreme commander of the British forces in 1778. Following the British evacuation of Boston in 1776, Hancock returned to his home on Beacon Hill, where he found the estate undamaged after the British occupancy.

Upon his return, Hancock became directly involved in politics and was elected to the Continental Congress as a representative from Massachusetts. He was later chosen as president of that Congress during the time when the Declaration of Independence was approved and was instrumental in mediating the differences between the then sovereign states during the convention and in convincing them to vote on the confederation. While in Boston, he hosted many social events at his home, including dinners for French naval officers and for the Marquis de Lafayette when he visited in 1778 and 1781.

In 1780, Hancock was elected the first governor of the Commonwealth of Massachusetts and was the guiding force in convincing the state legislature to approve the articles of the state constitution. He also worked with the other states, persuading them to join together in adopting the federal constitution. He continued as governor, interrupted only by the term of James Bowdoin, who was governor in 1786 and 1787.

While governor, Hancock entertained George Washington, who was on a tour of the states after his election as president in 1789. President Washington was traveling north toward Boston and stopped at Boston Neck awaiting an official greeting from the governor, but no Hancock was to be seen. A humorous anecdote regarding this visit is related by Bowditch in his Gleaner articles:

> *Governor Hancock thought that, as the Chief Magistrate of Massachusetts, it was not for him to take the first step, even when "The Father of our Country" visited us. He felt that his dignity, or, more properly, the dignity of the sovereign State which he represented, would be compromised by his making the first call, even on Washington. His Excellency, however, speedily discovered his mistake, and certainly took, or was supposed by the public to have taken, an ingenious mode of correcting it. Swathing his limbs in flannels—the victim of a sudden attack of the gout—he caused himself to* be carried *to visit the President* [by that time residing in his Boston Lodgings], *who, whatever may have been his private convictions, could not hesitate to accept and excuse the tardy civilities of such a suffering invalid.*[50]

Hancock was reelected after Bowdoin and continued as governor until his early death in 1793 at the age of fifty-six due to ill health, notably attributable to the gout. He had wanted to become the first president of the United States but realized that Washington was unbeatable. Therefore, he was willing to accept the vice presidency, but his ill health prevented him from championing his own cause. The post instead went to John Adams of Braintree.

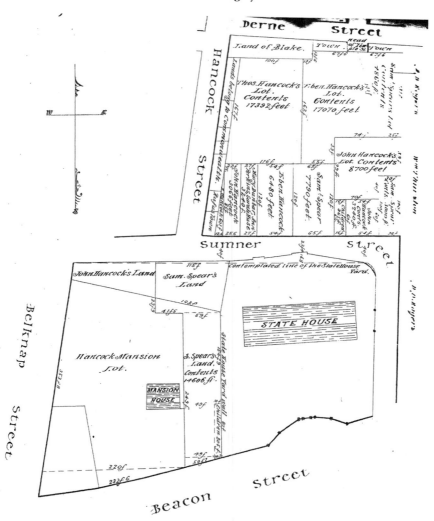

John Hancock estate division plan of 1819, showing the statehouse and the mansion house on the left.

Hancock lived in the house until his death and reportedly upon his deathbed was dictating a change in his will that would bequeath his mansion house to the commonwealth. Unfortunately, he died before his wishes could be carried out, thus preventing us from having a monument not only to the architecture of the times but also to one of the greatest Patriots of the American Revolution.

Following his death, his widow, Dorothy Quincy Hancock Scott (Mrs. Hancock had remarried, in 1796, one of Hancock's ship captains, James Scott), continued to live in the house until 1816. In 1821, she sold her dower rights to developer Israel Thorndike, who petitioned the court to partition the estate between himself and other legatees in order to develop the land. Thorndike was allocated a section with 102 feet on Beacon Street, which he sold to John Hubbard, who divided the land into lots that become 32, 33 and 34 Beacon. In 1826, the court partitioned the land under 31 Beacon to Samuel A. Eliot, while the eastern portion was allocated to Samuel Spear, who sold to Thorndike in 1819.

In 1819, the estate was divided. John Hancock's nephew (of the same name) retained ownership of the mansion house. He died in 1859, and according to his will, the property was not to be sold until four years after his death, when it was offered for sale at auction.

Many efforts were mounted to save this historic home, and the final attempt in 1863, the year of its razing, is considered the first effort in Boston of architectural conservation. It was proposed in the state legislature to dismantle the mansion and reassemble it elsewhere, and although Bostonians were in favor of this plan and would expend the funds, the rest of the commonwealth was not, being immersed in the struggles and costs of the Civil War.

As a result, in 1863 the mansion house and land were sold to James M. Beebe and Gardner Brewer, two successful Boston merchants who could not be convinced to preserve the house. The mansion was replaced by two large town houses erected by Beebe and Brewer in 1865 and initially numbered 30 and 30½ Beacon (later 29 and 30 Beacon). These houses were razed in 1917 to make way for the west wing of the statehouse.

The John Hancock House replica in Ticonderoga, New York, was built as the headquarters for the New York State Historical Association in 1926.

As late as 1926 there was an effort in the Massachusetts legislature to reproduce the house, but the issue "was disposed of February 4, 1926, following a lengthy hearing when the bill introduced by Representative George A. Anderson was referred to the next annual session of the legislature."[51] For some reason, the bill was never acted upon, so Boston and Massachusetts lost momentum for this memorial.

Fortunately, there is a replica of the original Hancock house in the historical town of Ticonderoga, New York. Constructed in 1926 by a Springfield paper industry merchant, Horace Augustus Moses, the reproduction was built as the headquarters for the New York State Historical Association. It was designed from measured drawings of the original building made by Boston architect John Hubbard Sturgis. "The exterior is a faithful copy, from the original plans...Inside, the two parlors to the right of the entrance and the main hall are copies of the corresponding rooms in the old house...The imposing stairway in the hall is an exact copy of the one in the old house."[52]

John Hancock's civic-minded intention of leaving his house upon his death to the commonwealth, for whose creation and existence he sacrificed so much, would eventually be fulfilled when the state took the land on which his mansion had stood and, in essence, utilized it for the common good in which Hancock so firmly believed.

29 (30) Beacon

This number was assigned to the eastern four-story brownstone double row house built by Gardner Brewer on the site of the John Hancock mansion.

Numbers 30 and 29 Beacon, the Beebe-Brewer double row house built on the site of John Hancock House, 1865. *Copyright © John F. Kennedy Library Foundation.*

Brewer and James Beebe had purchased the mansion house in 1863 at auction from the estate of John Hancock's nephew, and in the same year the famous stone house was razed after numerous attempts were made to preserve it. Brewer and Beebe then divided the property and built two connected large houses, with Beebe owning 30½ Beacon and Brewer residing in 30 Beacon—the same street number assigned to the Hancock House, which it replaced.

Brewer was the head of Gardner Brewer & Co., a commercial dry goods company located on Federal Street, and he lived at 23 Beacon Street until moving here in 1865.

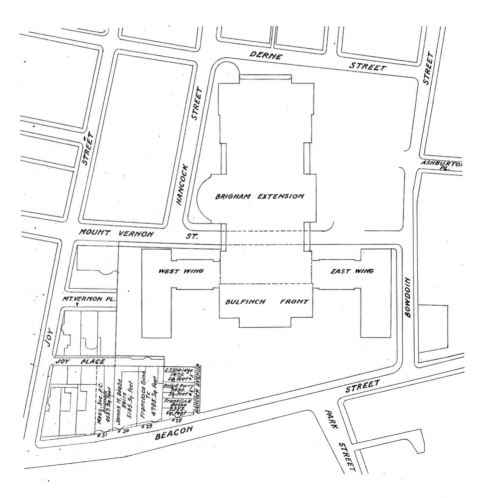

The 1916 plan of the Commonwealth of Massachusetts's taking of 31, 30, 29 and 28 Beacon.

The Brewer estate still owned the house as late as 1898 and in 1902 sold to Francesca G. Ginn of Ginn & Co., publishers. In 1916, the Commonwealth of Massachusetts took the building by eminent domain and razed the house, along with 28, 30 and 31 Beacon, to allow for expansion of the statehouse grounds and the addition of the new west wing.

Today, the site is the open grounds to the west of the statehouse where there are statues of President John F. Kennedy, Anne Hutchinson and Senator Henry Cabot Lodge

30 (30½) BEACON

This number was assigned to the western double row house constructed of brownstone by James M. Beebe on the site of the Hancock mansion.

James M. Beebe, along with Gardner Brewer, purchased the mansion house and the accompanying land in 1863 from the estate of John Hancock, the nephew of Governor John Hancock. Beebe was the owner of the largest wholesale dry goods business, both imported and domestic, in the country at the time. This dwelling, owned by Beebe, sat on a slightly larger lot than Brewer's house, and its "half" designation was the numbering practice of the time when two buildings replaced a single dwelling.

In 1916, the property, then owned by the James M. Beebe heirs, was taken by eminent domain by the Commonwealth of Massachusetts and razed to make way for the expansion of the statehouse grounds and the addition of the new west wing.

Today, the site is the open grounds on the western side of the Massachusetts Statehouse behind the plaque describing the former site of the John Hancock mansion.

31 BEACON

The house that once existed here was built on land that was part of Governor John Hancock's estate partitioned in 1826 by the Supreme Judicial Court of Massachusetts and allocated to Samuel A. Eliot, son of Samuel Eliot, who owned the mansion house at One Beacon.

This parcel was part of the land Samuel A. Eliot, along with Israel Thorndike, John Hubbard and others, acquired largely from Hancock's widow, Dorothy, and John Hancock, the nephew of the late governor.

Number 31 Beacon, circa 1870. It was removed in 1918. *Copyright © John F. Kennedy Library Foundation.*

Samuel Atkins Eliot was mayor of Boston for three years (1837–39) and a member of the United States Congress (1850–51). As mayor, he reorganized the city's fire departments with a higher state of efficiency and discipline. This followed the Broad Street Riot of 1837, when firemen, responding to an alarm, became embattled with an Irish funeral procession. Fighting broke out, and the riot was finally quelled when Eliot called in the military.

Samuel A. was the father of Charles Eliot, president of Harvard University, and also brother of William H. Eliot, the builder of the Tremont House Hotel. He was married to Mary Lyman, daughter of Theodore Lyman, who had this house designed and built by Cornelius Coolidge on Eliot's land and gave it to the newlyweds as a wedding present.

Eliot lived in the house until he lost his entire fortune in the Panic of 1857[53] as the result of poor investments. He subsequently sold the dwelling in 1858 to John E. Lodge, a merchant and father of Henry Cabot Lodge, the United States senator who served in the Senate from 1893 until his death in 1924. In 1905, the Lodge estate transferred the property to the Massachusetts Society for the Prevention of Cruelty to Animals, and in 1917 the Commonwealth of Massachusetts took the house by eminent domain and subsequently razed it.

32 (25) BEACON

This building replaced the house at 32 Beacon, built on land that was part of the original John Hancock estate.

Numbers 34 and 33 Beacon, with the new 25 Beacon on the right. Number 25 Beacon was the new headquarters for the American Unitarian Association, which was allowed to retain the address of Channing Hall.

Hancock's widow, Dorothy Quincy Hancock Scott, sold her interest in the estate in 1821 to Israel Thorndike. In 1823, Thorndike sold this land to John Hubbard, who then proceeded to divide the property into three lots facing the street at 32, 33 and 34 Beacon.

In 1825, Hubbard was assessed by the City of Boston for "three unfinished houses" designed by architect and builder Cornelius Coolidge, and in 1826 he sold this lot plus a new dwelling house to Mrs. Frances Hicks Rollins. Upon her husband Eben's death in 1833, Mrs. Rollins sold the property to the trustees of the Gardiner Greene estate.

The trustees purchased the house for the use of Mrs. Gardiner (Elizabeth C.) Greene, daughter of John Singleton Copley, the artist who had originally owned much of Beacon Hill. Mr. Greene died in 1832, and his famous residence on Pemberton Hill, with extensive gardens, was being sold. Mrs. Greene wanted to save a young ginkgo tree located on the grounds for which she had a special liking. Although it was difficult, the tree was moved to a spot opposite Mrs. Greene's new residence,[54] near the foot of the Gould Memorial Steps, where it stood until the 1970s. It was recently replaced by another tree, marked with a small plaque provided by the Friends of the Public Garden. Mrs. Greene lived here until her death at age ninety-six. In 1866, the house was purchased from her estate by Susan Jones Welles and Jane Welles.

In 1881, the house was sold by Susan Jones Welles to David Nevins of Tudor Apartments fame, and in 1886 Nevins sold to William Endicott, a partner in C.F. Hovey & Co., a large dry goods firm. In 1925, it was owned by the American Unitarian Association when it was razed to make way for the association's new headquarters.

Numbers 33 and 32
Beacon, circa 1870.
*Copyright © John F. Kennedy
Library Foundation.*

The association, celebrating its centennial in 1925, erected the present-day six-story structure in 1926, designed by Putnam & Cox, architects, and numbered it 25 Beacon in honor of its previous headquarters, replaced by the Hotel Bellevue in 1925. The original columns from the Endicott Mansion now flank the entryway, which is designed to resemble, if not duplicate, its predecessor.

Today, the building is the headquarters for the Unitarian Universalist Association, which was formed by the merger, in 1961, of the abovementioned American Unitarian Association and the Universalist Church of America.

33 BEACON

This house, designed by Cornelius Coolidge, was built on land that was part of the original Governor John Hancock estate and was sold by John Hubbard to Edward Tuckerman in 1826.

Edward was the father of Professor Edward Tuckerman of Amherst College, a noted lichenologist for whom Tuckerman's Ravine on Mt. Washington in New Hampshire—one of the most challenging downhill ski trails in the country—is named.

The house was sold in 1853 by Frederick Tuckerman to Eliza A. Parkman, widow of Dr. George Parkman, a physician and one of Boston's wealthiest men. Dr. Parkman had been gruesomely murdered in 1849 by Harvard chemistry professor John White Webster, a man who was in debt to him.

Webster knew the Parkman family well, and after denying involvement, he eventually confessed to and was found guilty of the murder following a lengthy and scandalous trial. During the time of the murder, the Parkmans' son, George Francis, had been living in Paris, and upon his return he moved his mother and sister here from their house on Walnut Street, where they could no longer bear to live.

George Francis and his sister lived the rest of their lives as unmarried recluses who were seldom seen in public. Upon his death in 1908, George Francis Parkman bequeathed his house to the City of Boston as part of his approximately $5 million endowment, "the income of which is to be applied to the maintenance and improvement of the Common and the Parks now existing."[55] Today, the house still belongs to the city and is often used by the mayor for meetings and receptions for special guests. The building appears today much as it did in the middle of the nineteenth century.

A tablet on the building states:

HERE LIVED AND DIED
GEORGE F. PARKMAN
1823–1908
REMEMBERED WITH ENDURING
GRATITUDE BY THE CITY OF
BOSTON FOR HIS BEQUEST OF
A FUND THAT SECURES FOR
EVER THE MAINTENANCE AND
IMPROVEMENT OF THE COMMON
AND OTHER PUBLIC PARKS

34 BEACON

This much-altered house was erected by Cornelius Coolidge[56] in 1824 on part of the original Governor John Hancock estate and was sold by John Hubbard in 1826 to Nathaniel Pope Russell, a State Street marine insurance broker.

Russell sold the house in 1850 to James Bowdoin Bradlee, merchant, whose business, Josiah Bradlee & Co., was on Central Wharf. In 1878, the Bradlee estate sold the property to Susan B. Cabot, who retained ownership for over thirty years.

In 1909, Cabot sold the residence to Charles W. Allen, who four years later, in 1913, sold to Little, Brown & Co., a respected Boston publishing

Numbers 34 and 33 Beacon, circa 1865. *Courtesy of the Bostonian Society/Old State House Museum.*

firm founded in 1837. The firm published many famous authors, including Emily Dickinson, Louisa May Alcott, Ogden Nash and Gore Vidal, among many others. It retained the building as its headquarters until 1997, when the premises were converted once again into a private residence. The building's appearance on the side facing Beacon Street is today much like it was in the middle of the nineteenth century, but the rear has been substantially modified.

Today, the property is owned by Northeastern University and is used as the home of its president.

7

JOY STREET TO
WALNUT STREET

34½ BEACON

This nine-story residential building, the high-rise Tudor Apartments, stands on the site of Dr. John Joy's wooden mansion house that was designed by Charles Bulfinch and erected in 1791.

Joy, whose brother Benjamin was a member of the Mount Vernon Proprietors, had acquired various parcels of land that composed his estate bordering on Beacon Street, Walnut Street on the west and on the east Belknap Street, later renamed Joy Street in his honor. His title—"Doctor"—was often applied to apothecaries of the day.

In 1792, a traveler gave the following description of the house:

> *The front is among the neatest and most elegant I have seen. It is two stories high, overcast, and painted a kind of peach-bloom color, and adorned with semi-columns, fluted, of Corinthian order, the whole height of the edifice.*[57]

After Joy's death in 1813, his widow, Abigail, continued to live there until 1832, when she moved to Mount Vernon Street. The estate was sold in 1833 to Israel Thorndike. The Bulfinch House was then dismantled and moved to South Boston Point to the land of Benjamin Adams, where it was reerected.

Thorndike proceeded to develop the vacant land into three house lots (thirty-four and a half, thirty-five and thirty-six). On the corner lot, thirty-four and a half, he built a large house (with the entrance on Walnut Street),

Left: Tudor Apartments, 34½ Beacon, now condominiums.

Below: John Joy House, designed by Charles Bulfinch and removed in 1833 to South Boston. *Courtesy Boston Athenaeum*.

which he occupied himself. He did not stay there long; in 1838, he sold the property to Robert Gould Shaw, son of the Revolutionary War soldier Francis Shaw.

Robert Gould Shaw was a successful businessman and participated in the development of what is now East Boston and in the building of the steamship pier for the Cunard Lines. He was the grandfather of the Civil War hero of the same name, and upon his and his wife's deaths in 1853, the estate was sold by their heirs to Frederick Tudor.

Tudor, a merchant, made his fortune exporting one of New England's natural products—ice—which he placed in insulated ships

Tudor House, circa 1870, built by Frederick Tudor, the "Ice King." *Courtesy of the Bostonian Society/Old State House Museum.*

and sent to destinations in the Caribbean, California and as far away as India. His worldwide shipping operated from Tudor Wharf, an eighteenth-century structure that he purchased in 1874.

Tudor lived in his Beacon Street mansion house until his demise in 1864, and his widow continued to reside in the house until her death in 1884.

The estate was sold in 1885 to David Nevins, a developer, whose family was in banking. He removed the mansion house and in its place erected, between 1885 and 1887, a nine-story apartment house designed by architect S.J.F. Thayer known as the Tudor Apartments. The construction of this building caused a furor on Beacon Hill, as many residents were deprived of their favored view of the golden dome of the Massachusetts Statehouse. This outcry from the controversy led to the imposition of building height restrictions in the city. Thayer also designed the original Jordan Marsh Department store building on Washington Street that was demolished in 1972.

David Nevins's heirs still retained ownership of the property as late as 1957, when they sold the building to the Family Service Association of Greater Boston, which for many years utilized the building as its headquarters.

Today, the property is again being used for residences, as the building has been converted into luxury condominiums retaining much of its original exterior design.

35 BEACON

This mostly original house was erected on a parcel of land that was part of the Joy estate sold by the Joy heirs in 1833 to Israel Thorndike.

Thorndike subdivided the land, and this site was sold in 1834 to Samuel T. Armstrong, who built a house in 1835. Armstrong was a printer and book publisher by profession, specializing in religious publications. In 1820, his firm published *Scott's Family Bible* in six volumes and was "one of the earliest instances of stereotyping on a large scale in America."[58] Armstrong, who was the son of the Revolutionary War soldier John Armstrong, had been a captain in the War of 1812.

Numbers 36 and 35 Beacon, 1870. *Courtesy of the Bostonian Society/Old State House Museum.*

He was elected lieutenant governor of Massachusetts in 1834 and in 1835 became acting governor of the state when Governor John Davis went to the United States Senate. In 1836, Armstrong was elected mayor of Boston, and as such he oversaw construction of the courthouse in Court Square and the erection of the iron fence surrounding the Boston Common.

As late as 1882, the house was still occupied by Abigail Armstrong, who sold the same year to Thomas Burnham, a successful dealer in antiques and books. In 1892, Burnham sold the house to David Nevins, who also owned the adjacent apartment house, 34½ Beacon.

This house today appears much as it did when Armstrong occupied it, except for the addition of an attic floor and a change to the entrance stairs, which were moved to below grade level. The original entrance is now a set of French doors opening onto a small balcony situated above the new entrance. The building retains its early nineteenth-century reserved façade of brick and large windows.

Nevins's heirs retained possession of the house until 1958, when they sold the property to Anna M. Crocker. Today, the building houses five condominium units.

36 BEACON

This mostly original house was built on the westernmost parcel of the John Joy estate that Israel Thorndike sold in 1833 to Benjamin C. Clarke, who erected a house designed by architect and builder Cornelius Coolidge. Clarke was a West India merchant and shipowner with offices at Commercial Wharf. He was also the author of a pamphlet describing Hayti (Haiti), a country with which he had considerable business relations.

In 1862, Clarke sold the house, and in 1899 Melvin O. Adams was the owner. As late as 1938, the Adams heirs remained the owners. At one time, Melvin Adams was owner of Middle Brewster Island in Boston Harbor.

This house appears much as it did when it was originally built, even retaining the nineteenth-century wrought-iron balustrade in front of the large windows on the second floor.

The major changes to the façade included the relocation of the main entrance from the first floor down to the street level, thereby eliminating the front steps—a common alteration that utilized the ground floor as living space. There is also a small attic-floor addition typical to many preserved yet renovated houses along Beacon Street.

At present, the building houses eight condominium units.

37 BEACON (OLD NUMBER)

The mansion house that was originally here was constructed by Samuel Appleton on a lot measuring forty-three feet on Beacon Street that had been part of the John Joy estate. This desirable lot of land near the corner of Beacon and Walnut Streets, overlooking the Boston Common, was sold in 1806 to Uriah Cotting, a real estate developer.

Cotting, who was called by Bowditch in his Gleaner series the "Chief Benefactor of Boston,"[59] was the inspiration behind the creation of the Mill Dam in 1813, upon which was constructed Western Avenue (Beacon Street), which opened to traffic in 1821. The construction of the Mill Dam by the Boston & Roxbury Mill Corporation led to the eventual laying out and filling in of Back Bay.

Cotting was one of the wealthiest men in Boston at that time and started the construction of an imposing mansion on this site. However, by the time the first floor had been completed, the War of 1812 had started, and this, along with the effects of the Jeffersonian Embargo, proved disastrous to his real estate investments. This downturn caused Cotting to dispose of much of his real estate holdings and forced him to halt construction of his house. He later removed the partially built house and in 1816 sold the vacant land now consisting of two parcels. He sold the western portion of this land, 38 Beacon, to Benjamin P. Homer. In 1818, he sold the eastern portion, 37 Beacon, upon which Cotting had begun construction of his large mansion, to Samuel Appleton.

Appleton had moved to Boston from New Hampshire in 1794 and had opened a shop in Cornhill selling rum and other goods. The business was so successful that he brought in his younger brother, Nathan (later owner of 54 Beacon Street), to be his partner. Samuel pursued the importing business and for many years lived in London, where he purchased textiles to send to Boston for sale. At the time of the War of 1812, he was already very rich. He was also involved in the development of the textile factories that were built along the Merrimack River and in early Massachusetts railroad investments.

He was a bachelor until 1819, when at the age of fifty-two he married Mary Lekain Gore, a widow. Appleton then constructed on the land purchased from Cotting a large mansion house covering the site, and although there is no picture available today, there is a likeness of the building engraved on a silver pitcher that Samuel's brother Nathan commissioned upon Samuel's death.[60]

Samuel was a generous contributor to the needy and was considered a philanthropist in the true Boston tradition, giving away an estimated half of his income yearly.[61] He was elected to the Massachusetts legislature and later was a presidential elector who voted for Daniel Webster in 1836. Coincidentally, his nephew, Samuel Appleton, son of his brother Eben, married Webster's daughter, Julia, in 1839.

After Samuel's death in 1853, his widow proceeded to sell the property at public auction in 1856 and subsequently moved to 53 Beacon, which Samuel had purchased in 1816. John A. Blanchard, the buyer at auction, then razed the old house and divided the property into two lots, upon which he built a double brownstone row house numbered 37 and 37½ Beacon.

37 BEACON (NEW NUMBER)

This new 37 Beacon was assigned to the easterly brownstone house built by John A. Blanchard and sold in 1858 to John Borland. In 1882, the property was sold by Alida Borland to Arthur T. Lyman.

Numbers 38, 37½, 37 and 36 Beacon circa 1875. Numbers 37 and 37½ Beacon are an excellent example of mirror-image double row houses. *Copyright © John F. Kennedy Library Foundation.*

The new 37 Beacon replaced 38, 37½ and 37 Beacon. A portion of 36 Beacon can be seen at right.

Lyman had varying financial interests, including textile mills. He was the president of the Pacific Mills and the Bigelow Carpet Co. and proprietor of the company that owned the locks and canals on the Merrimack River. He was also a trustee of the Provident Institute for Savings and president of the Boston Athenaeum.

In 1884, Lyman sold the house to Sarah P.L. (Lowell) Blake, whose heirs sold the property (along with 37½ Beacon) in 1939 to a real estate company, Thirty-eight Beacon, Inc., which also purchased 38 Beacon.

The three residences, 37, 37½ and 38 Beacon—all then owned by Thirty-eight Beacon, Inc.—were razed in 1940 and in their place a New York–style apartment house, now 37 Beacon, was erected. It exists today much as it did when it was originally built. This apartment house, designed by architect Herman L. Feer, has six floors and originally included thirty-five apartments.

The building was converted to condominiums in the 1980s and today is a desirable doorman building, an unusual amenity for Beacon Hill residences.

37½ BEACON

This number, 37½ Beacon, was the address of the westerly brownstone double row house built by John A. Blanchard and sold in 1857 to Freeman Allen, of Freeman, Harris and Potter, boots, shoe and leather dealers. Allen then sold the property in 1863 to Isaac Rich, fish merchant and one of the founders of Boston University (BU), who left his considerable fortune to BU upon his death.[62]

In 1872, the property was transferred through Rich's trustee, William Claflin, to Bessie Winthrop, and in 1893 Robert C. Winthrop Jr. sold the house to Sarah P.L. Blake. In 1928, the building housed the YWCA Business Women's Branch.[63]

These residences, plus 37 and 38 Beacon (new number), were sold in 1939 to Thirty-eight Beacon, Inc., which subsequently razed the buildings in 1940 to make way for a New York–style apartment house.

38 BEACON

The house that had this address was built on the westerly portion of land purchased from John Joy by Uriah Cotting in 1806. After Cotting's financial reversals, he sold this parcel of land in 1816 to Benjamin P. Homer, successful private underwriter and East India merchant, who then erected a house on the lot.[64]

In 1857, Nancy B. Homer, the widow of Fitzhenry Homer (Benjamin's son), who had been the agent at the time for the Argentine Republic, offered the estate for sale at auction at the same time as the adjacent Samuel Appleton House. In 1857, James Lawrence, of the dry goods firm of Amos & Abbot Lawrence, purchased the house and proceeded to remodel it, making alterations that included changing the entrance from the first floor to the basement level (see photo in "37 Beacon (New Number)").

In 1882, James transferred the property to A. Lawrence Winthrop, and in 1939 the estate sold the house to Thirty-eight Beacon, Inc. It, along with 37 and 37½ Beacon, was razed in 1940 to make way for a thirty-five-unit apartment house now numbered 37 Beacon.

8

COPLEY ESTATE

The estate of John Singleton Copley comprised over eighteen acres of land and was acquired by Copley between the years of 1769 and 1773. Copley, who was born in 1738 in Boston, was considered by many to be the foremost portrait artist of colonial America and was most sought out by many important citizens of Massachusetts and New York. He was known for using the device of including with the portrait articles that would normally be used by the subject. For example, in his portrait of Paul Revere, owned by the Museum of Fine Arts in Boston, he showed the Patriot holding one of his silver teapots. Copley had studios in both New York and Boston, where he remodeled the Lower Copley House to suit his needs.

Copley had purchased his land from the original estates of Blackstone, Sewall and East. Its boundaries were the Boston Common to the south, Walnut Street to the east, Mount Vernon Street to the north (including what is now Louisburg Square) and the low-water mark of the Charles River to the west.[65] Along Beacon Street, the southern boundary would extend from today's Walnut Street westward to 87 Beacon.

The property included three houses, as shown in the Christian Remick watercolor of 1768, *A Perspective View of Part of the Common.* These buildings are known as Upper Copley House, Lower Copley House and an additional structure whose use was unknown.

Copley left Boston for London in 1774 at the urging of the American painter Benjamin West, who had already migrated there. He advised that there were many more notables in London who wanted their portraits done than he could ever find in America. After relocating to England,

Copley Estate, 1768. Watercolor by Christian Remick showing, from left, the Lower Copley House and Upper Copley House. To the right is the John Hancock House, with Beacon Hill and the beacon beyond.

Copley decided to sell his land on Beacon Hill, as the value was increasing along with the population of the town. His agent for this purpose was Gardiner Greene, Esq., who was married to Copley's daughter, Elizabeth. Greene entered into an agreement to sell the eighteen-acre estate—comprising approximately eleven acres of upland and seven acres of flats—to Jonathan Mason Jr. and Harrison Gray Otis, representing the Mount Vernon Proprietors (MVP), for $18,450.

Coincidentally, Otis was on a committee to select a site for the new statehouse, which had chosen Beacon Hill as its location. It seems evident, therefore, that Otis and Mason were aware that Copley's property would increase in value as a result of its proximity to the new statehouse. When Copley discovered the impending construction of the new statehouse adjacent to his estate, he attempted to rescind the contract, claiming that he should have been advised of this development. Realizing that the contract was legally binding, he sent as his agent his son, John Singleton Copley Jr., who later became Lord Chancellor Lyndhurst in England, to sign the contract and consummate the sale.

Copley Estate

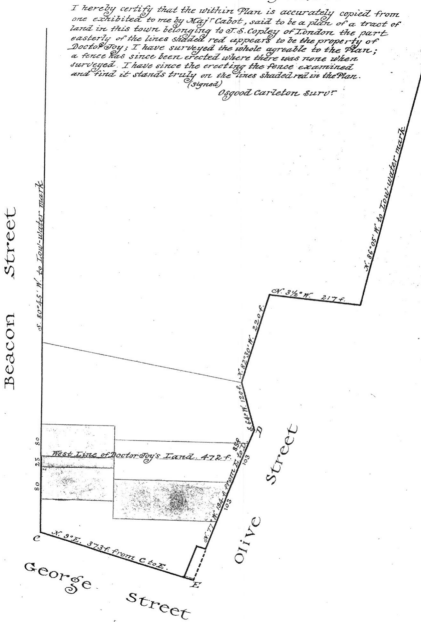

Boston, July 7, 1794.

I hereby certify that the within Plan is accurately copied from
one exhibited to me by Maj.ʳ Cabot, said to be a plan of a tract of
land in this town belonging to J.S.Copley of London the part
easterly of the lines shaded red appears to be the property of
Doctoʳ Joy; I have surveyed the whole agreable to the Plan;
a fence has since been erected where there was none when
surveyed. I have since the erecting the fence examined
and find it stands truly on the lines shaded red in the Plan.
(signed)
Osgood Carleton Surv.ʳ

Beacon Street

S. 80°45' W. to low-water mark

N. 86°05' W. to low-water mark

N. 3½° W. 217 f.

N. 82°30' W. 220 f.

S. 64° W. 120 f.

West Line of Doctor Joy's Land. 472 f.

Olive Street

C

N. 9° E. 373 f. from C to E.

George Street

D

E

85 ¢
103

N. 77 W. 104 f. from E to D
103

80
25
80

The 1794 plan showing the area of Copley's land sale to the Mount Vernon
Proprietors. George Street, later Hancock Street, was removed with the expansion of
the statehouse grounds.

Although potential for development of the approximately eleven acres of upland was fairly evident, the unknown potential for the approximately seven acres of tidal flats to be filled and then developed was not so obvious. There must have been thoughts of possible use for the submerged land, however, as reference made to this part of the purchase was delineated in the document of sale. The description of the property line toward the Charles River Basin states, "Lastly by a line running Northwesterly toward the water, together with all the flatts [sic] lying before the same down to low water mark,"[66] which was approximately 850 feet west from Walnut Street.

This description allowed the MVP, between the 1820s and 1830s, to fill and build on these flats as far as today's 87 Beacon, bringing the total buildable acreage of the Copley purchase to almost nineteen acres.

The purchase and subsequent development of this land by the MVP changed Beacon Hill and Beacon Street from a sparsely inhabited area to the most desirable address in Boston in an amazingly short period of time. The proprietors were not only smart and responsible businesspeople but also had a desire to build homes that would endure both physically and aesthetically, a goal that they most certainly accomplished.

9

MOUNT VERNON
PROPRIETORS

The Mount Vernon Proprietors (MVP) was a syndicate formed in 1794 for the purpose of purchasing, developing and selling real estate in the relatively unpopulated West End of the town of Boston, primarily in the Beacon Street and Beacon Hill areas.

The original proprietors were Harrison Gray Otis, mayor of Boston, United States congressman and senator from Massachusetts; Jonathan Mason, also a U.S. congressman and senator; William Scollay, a retired apothecary; Joseph Woodward, a merchant; and Charles Bulfinch, an architect.[67]

This is the group that purchased the Copley Lands in 1796 and started the real estate development that encompassed not only the south slope of Beacon Hill but also a large majority of what was to become known as the Back Bay. They laid out lots and streets using names of trees, such as Walnut, Spruce and Cedar, similar to what had been done in Philadelphia, while using names of well-known Federalists for more important streets, such as Pinckney and Revere.[68] The proprietors also laid out Louisburg Square and created the beautiful park that exists there today.

The list of members soon changed, however. In 1797, Bulfinch sold out to Benjamin Joy, brother of Dr. John Joy, and the Woodward and Scollay interests were purchased by Otis, Mason and Mrs. James (Hepzibah Clarke) Swan.

Mrs. Swan was the wife of Colonel James Swan, who participated in the Boston Tea Party and fought at the Battle of Bunker Hill. The Swans were in France at the start of the French Revolution but returned home before encountering trouble themselves. Colonel Swan, however, returned to France, where he made a considerable fortune, which he sent back to his wife. Remaining in France, he was arrested in 1815 and sent to debtors' prison, as he had refused to let his wife pay his debts.[69] He stayed in prison until pardoned by Louis Philippe in 1830 but died before he could return home.

Mrs. Swan's interests were represented for a time by General Henry Jackson and, later, a son-in-law, William Sullivan, who acted as trustees for her. Jackson was "formerly colonel of the Sixteenth Continental Regiment, [and] was appointed naval agent by his bosom friend, General Henry Knox, when the latter was Secretary of War"[70] under George Washington. Jackson was naval agent when the frigate USS *Constitution* was being built at Edmund Hartt's shipyard in Boston.

At the time of the Copley land purchase, the shoreline of the Charles River was located approximately where 62 Beacon Street is today. All the area west of that has been filled, or made land, and most of that was created through the efforts of the proprietors.

As the result of a number of agreements, the proprietors divided ownership of the lands they purchased, with each possessing parcels to do with as they pleased. This included the lands from Joy Street west to the Charles River Basin, the newly completed Charles Street and the windfall of the Back Bay flats.

The filling of the basin started around 62 Beacon and ended with Charles Street, which was created with material primarily brought down from

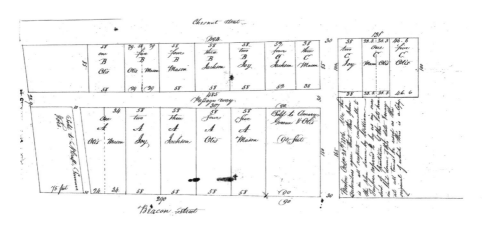

The 1806 plan of the Mount Vernon Proprietors' division of Copley's land shows how 50–64 Beacon were allocated. *Courtesy of Historic New England.*

Mount Vernon by a gravity railroad, considered the first such conveyance in use in the United States. At the same time that Charles Street was laid out in 1803, abutments were created to keep the filled land from washing into the Charles River. The proprietors then continued filling beyond the western side of Charles Street to an additional one hundred feet to the west, ending in a wharf in the Charles River. Building then stopped until an agreement was reached between the proprietors and the Boston & Roxbury Mill Corporation allowing the construction of buildings on the north side of the Mill Dam Road, later Western Avenue and then Beacon Street.

The Boston & Roxbury Mill Corporation gave the MVP, in an indenture dated January 6, 1824, permission to utilize the dam (and road)[71] as a southerly wall for its project of filling in the flats and erecting buildings thereupon.

This agreement was the original basis for the filling in of Back Bay and the creation of the architectural treasures we still have today.

Walnut Street to Spruce Street

Phillips-Winthrop House

This mansion house, one of the two oldest existing houses on Beacon Street, was the first dwelling erected on land sold by John Singleton Copley to the Mount Vernon Proprietors (MVP). The property, which had been allocated to Jonathan Mason by a 1799 Mount Vernon Proprietors partition of lands, was sold in 1804 to John Phillips, who the same year built this brick house attributed to Charles Bulfinch. The original appearance of the house can be seen on the far left of the Richie engraving of the Boston Common.

In 1822, Boston changed its government from a town to a city,[72] and that year Phillips was elected the first mayor, with little opposition after Harrison Gray Otis and Josiah Quincy withdrew their names as candidates.

Phillips's accomplishments as mayor revolved around the creation of municipal departments in the newly formed city. He was able to serve only a one-year term because of poor health, and he died the following year. He was the father of Wendell Phillips, the famous and devoted antislavery orator who was born in the house in 1811.

Wendell was a follower of William Lloyd Garrison, the abolitionist, and after the Civil War he used his oratory skills to champion other causes, such as women's suffrage, Prohibition and prison reform. A statue honoring him, sculpted by Daniel Chester French, stands in the Public Garden on the Boylston Street Mall. French, a noted sculptor, also created the George Robert

Phillips-Winthrop House, erected 1804. This was the first house built on the Mount Vernon Proprietors land purchased from John Singleton Copley.

White sculpture fountain in the Public Garden at the corner of Beacon and Arlington Streets and the Abraham Lincoln sculpture in the Lincoln Memorial in Washington, D.C.

The estate was sold by the Phillips heirs in 1825 to Thomas Lindall Winthrop, lieutenant governor of Massachusetts from 1826 to 1832 and a descendant of Massachusetts Bay Company governor John Winthrop.

Mr. Winthrop, having a large family, increased the size of the house while changing the original roofline and the location for the main entrance from Beacon Street to 1 Walnut Street, which is its address today. During his term as lieutenant governor, the city celebrated the 200th anniversary of its founding with parades and celebrations, including a visit to the city by then ex-president John Quincy Adams, who attended a reception at Winthrop's home.[73]

Winthrop died in 1841, and the estate was sold that year to Thomas Dixon, merchant and the Dutch consul at Boston. He lived there until his death in 1849, and in 1861 the mansion was owned by Robert M. Mason, a partner of Amos Adams Lawrence, the textile magnate. Mason occupied the house until his death in 1879, when the house was conveyed to his daughters, the Misses Ellen and Ida Mason. In 1930, the estate of Ellen F. Mason sold the house to Helen O. Storrow, a noted philanthropist, whose husband, James, was honored with the naming of Storrow Drive.

The next year, 1931, Storrow conveyed the property to the Judge Baker Foundation, named in honor of the Boston Juvenile Court's first judge, Harvey Humphrey Baker. As described in the center's history statement, "The Center embodied the ideals of a revolutionary group of child psychologists who felt that it was more constructive to support rather than punish, 'wayward' and delinquent children." The center remained on Beacon Hill until 1957, when it moved to Boston's Longwood Medical area, where it still continues its programs.

Today, the Phillips-Winthrop House is used for offices.

39 BEACON

This brick mansion was built on the site of the Upper Copley House, one of three wooden houses[74] fronting on Beacon Street belonging to the estate of John Singleton Copley when sold to the MVP in 1796.

The Upper Copley House, located between John Phillips's land on the east and the Lower Copley House of John Vinal on the west, was sold by the proprietors in 1796 to Charles Cushing, the clerk of the Massachusetts Supreme Court. In 1816, his children sold the estate to Nathan Appleton and Daniel P. Parker, business partners in a textile and dry goods business that they had started in 1810. It was Appleton, along with Francis C. Lowell, who introduced the power (textile) loom to the United States

Numbers 41, 40 and 39 Beacon.

Numbers 40 and 39 Beacon, circa 1870, built in 1816. A fourth floor was added in 1888. *Courtesy of Historic New England.*

and recommended renaming the town where the textile mills were to be erected from East Chelmsford to Lowell.

After purchasing the property, Appleton and Parker demolished the Cushing House and proceeded to build a brick double row house—39 Beacon, where Appleton, who was then living at 54 Beacon Street, was to reside, and 40 Beacon, where Parker would live. The houses were designed by Alexander Parris, whose Federal style is still beautiful today.

For many years, the house was a social center, as many of Nathan's eight children became notable in their own right. His daughter Frances (Fanny) married poet Henry Wadsworth Longfellow (in the front rooms of 39 Beacon) and a son, Thomas Gold Appleton, became famous as a painter and writer.

Appleton served from 1831 to 1833 as a United States congressman and again in 1842. Following his retirement from Congress, he continued his business interests. He lived in this house from its completion in 1819 until his death in 1861, and his second wife, Harriet Coffin Sumner Appleton, continued to live in the house, surviving him by six years. She left the house to her two sons, Nathan and William Sumner, who sold the property in 1886 to Arthur T. Lyman, who was also in the textile business and a director of the Boston Manufacturing Company.

The houses were enlarged in 1888, when a fourth floor designed by architects Hartwell and Richardson was added, including a third bay window on each floor.

In 1940, Ronald T. Lyman sold the house to the Women's City Club, which was formed "to promote acquaintance among women through their common interest in the welfare of the City of Boston and the Commonwealth of Massachusetts; to maintain an open forum in matters of public import and civic interest may be heard frequently."[75] The club also provided dining rooms, function rooms and bedrooms and occupied the property as its headquarters from the 1940s until the 1990s, when it was converted back to residential use.

40 Beacon

This brick mansion, along with 39 Beacon, was built on the site of the Upper Copley House in 1816 by Daniel Pinckney Parker, along with Nathan Appleton, his business partner. This residence was an identical mirror image in exterior design to 39 Beacon but had an interior that was more ornate,[76] reflecting Parker's somewhat less conservative style. Beacon Street was increasingly becoming the most fashionable part of town, and many visiting dignitaries would parade down the street. President Andrew Jackson visited Boston in 1833 to attend the opening of a new dry dock at the Charlestown Navy Yard, and while promenading on Beacon Street, he had not been receiving the adulation expected. He passed by the window of Parker's house, and while his daughter was seen waving her handkerchief from the window, Parker himself was ignoring Jackson. Such was the feeling of many Bostonians.[77]

Although Parker's business partnership with Appleton ended during the War of 1812, he remained a successful merchant and also was, for several years, trustee of the Massachusetts General Hospital.[78] Upon his death, "he owned one of the finest vessels in the port to which he had given the name of his friend and neighbor, *Samuel Appleton*."[79]

In 1852, the Parker family sold the house to Henderson Inches, a successful merchant and owner at the time of India Wharf. The house was modified in 1888, as was 39 Beacon, by the addition of a fourth floor. This house, however, retained the original design of two windows in the bay on each floor.

The property remained in the Inches family until 1901, when George B. Inches sold the house to David W. Emery, an interior designer. The home was offered for sale by Emery in 1913 and is featured in the August 1913 edition of the *Bulletin of the Society for the Preservation of New England Antiquities*. In the issue, the society states that "the interior of the house is considered by almost all who have seen it the most beautiful in Boston."

The article also says that for many years people thought the house was designed by Charles Bulfinch and that it might be demolished to make way for a "a high apartment house," probably referring to what had happened with 48 Beacon. They expressed hope that some society (such as SPNEA, now Historic New England, if it could raise the funds) might decide to purchase the building for its headquarters. Although SPNEA did not purchase the house, it was fortunately never demolished. It was eventually sold to an association that respected its history, the Women's City Club, which purchased it in 1919 and occupied it until the 1990s.

Today, the house has been converted back into residences.

41 BEACON

This brick house was built on land that was purchased by the MVP and included the existing Lower Copley House. The proprietors sold it in 1796 to John Vinal, a justice of the peace and schoolmaster of the South Writing School, known as the Schoolhouse on the Common, as it was located on West Street near the Common.

Numbers 43, 42 and 41 Beacon. The entrance to 43 Beacon is hidden to the left of the Common stairway.

Vinal sold the property in 1818 to David Sears the younger, including the land on which Sears was to build 42 Beacon. This house, 41 Beacon, was built in 1839 by Sears for his daughter, Harriet Dickson Sears, and her husband, George Caspar Crowninshield, son of Benjamin W. Crowninshield, Madison's secretary of war. Sears retained ownership of the house while the Crowninshields lived here, and in 1852 Sears's son-in-law, William Amory, and his family moved here from 43 Beacon. Sears retained ownership until his death in 1871, when the estate transferred ownership to Anna S. Amory.

The building remained in the Amory family until it was sold in 1897 by Francis D. Amory to the Somerset Club, thereby giving the club ownership of the entire former Sears estate of 41, 42 and 43 Beacon. This building appears much the same today as it did when it was first built. It presently houses eight condominiums.

42 Beacon

This stone mansion was constructed on land that was part of the Copley estate purchased by the MVP and sold in 1796 to John Vinal.

At that time, there was a wooden house on the site that had been erected by Silvester Gardiner, an apothecary, who in 1746 purchased the land that was originally part of the Sewalls' Elm Pasture. The house was purchased in 1770 by Copley, who altered it considerably to use as an artist's studio under the direction of Copley's half brother, Henry Pelham, an architect and cartographer. On the wall bordering Beacon Street a tablet states:

> *On this site*
> *stood the home of*
> *John Singleton Copley*
> *distinguished historical and*
> *portrait painter*
> *born in Boston 1737*
> *died in London 1815*

Copley left Boston in 1774 and moved permanently to London. Until the sale of his estate, the property was rented to various tenants, including General Henry Knox, Washington's secretary of war, who resided here for a period after the Revolutionary War.[80]

David Sears House, as originally designed by Alexander Parris in 1822, with the main entrance facing east. *Courtesy of Harvard University Archives HUC8782.514(253).*

In 1818, John Vinal sold the property, which measured ninety feet on Beacon Street, for $20,000 to David Sears, who tore down the wooden house and began the construction of the stone mansion house. Completed in 1822, this house, which was designed by Alexander Parris, still exists today, although in a much modified form.[81] Parris, whose designs include St. Paul's Church on Tremont Street, the Lyman House on the corner of Joy and Mt. Vernon Streets and Quincy Market, became, with the construction of the Sears House, a recognized architect of substantial note in Boston.

The size of the house was nearly doubled in 1831 as Sears bought the adjoining westerly lot from Harrison Gray Otis and erected a three-story granite house. This house was constructed with a bay resembling the one at 42 Beacon, and at the same time he added a third story to his mansion and combined the two dwellings. Along with Parris, architect Solomon Willard assisted in the carving of the marble panels on the front of the house and also on the adjoining 43 Beacon. Willard also worked on the Tremont House Hotel and was the architect of the Bunker Hill Monument.

In 1838, Sears furthered his building on Beacon Street by erecting 41 Beacon, which was a present to his daughter Harriet, who married George Caspar Crowninshield. This building's site, to the east of 42 Beacon, necessitated moving the main entrance of Sears's house from its original location on the east side of the mansion to Beacon Street and eliminated the windows on the east side of the house.

David Sears was born in 1787 in his father's house at the corner of Beacon and Somerset Streets and lived there until building his mansion. He married Miriam Clarke Mason, the daughter of Jonathan Mason, United States senator and a partner of the MVP. Sears, often addressed as colonel, was a philanthropist and was involved in financing the building of St. Paul's Church in 1820. He also generously set up the Sears Fund to benefit the building. His involvement with many charities was well known, including the Fifty Associates Charity, of which he was a member and whose income went to the Overseers of the Poor.

He had inherited a large fortune from his father and spent much of his time managing its affairs and making real estate investments. While traveling in Europe between 1811 and 1814 with Miriam, he resided in Paris during the celebrations accompanying the birth of Napoleon's son, and he and his wife were introduced to the Empress Josephine, with whom they developed a mutual affection. The original doorway of 42 Beacon had two marble vases in her memory that had come from Malmaison, Josephine's residence outside of Paris, where she lived after the annulment of her marriage to Napoleon in 1823.[82]

The Searses entertained extensively, and many famous personages found their way to 42 Beacon, including Alexis de Tocqueville and his traveling companion, Beaumont, who visited them in 1831 and subsequently wrote, "We dined the other day at Mr. Sears'. He has a fortune of five or six millions, his house is a kind of palace, he reigns there in great luxury, he treated us with splendor, I have never anywhere seen dinners more sumptuous."[83] Later in life, Sears became a republican and was a great supporter of Lincoln and his antislavery cause. Upon a visit to Boston, Sears entertained President-elect Ulysses S. Grant at a banquet held at his home.

After Sears's death in 1871, the mansion was sold by the estate to the present owner, the Somerset Club, which at the same time acquired the house Sears had built at 43 Beacon. After moving here, the club proceeded to modify the houses for its purposes, with the architectural firm of Snell and Gregerson providing plans for the numerous alterations. At one time, the club had many sports facilities, including a badminton court and even a bowling alley.[84] The club also acquired 41 Beacon in 1896, giving it the three contiguous Sears houses at 41, 42 and 43 Beacon.

43 BEACON

This house was built on a site that was part of the eleven acres purchased in 1795 by Otis and Mason from Copley and allocated to Harrison Gray Otis under the 1799 MVP's Agreement of Partition.

The lot was originally laid out as part of the garden to the east of Harrison Gray Otis's mansion-house, 45 Beacon, built in 1805. By 1831, Otis thought that "land at last became so valuable that he did not feel justified in retaining for a mere matter of sentiment this beautiful [garden] enclosure, which had long pleased all eyes, and decided to convert it to a more substantial use."[85]

As a result, he decided to sell, in 1831, the eastern half of his garden, measuring twenty-five feet, on Beacon Street to his neighbor, David Sears. On this lot, Sears built for his daughter, Anna, and her husband, William Amory, a three-story granite house that was actually an addition to his adjacent mansion house.

Amory, who was treasurer of the Amoskeag Company, one of the nation's largest textile manufacturers, lived here with his family until 1852, when they moved to 41 Beacon. After their departure, the house was occupied by another Sears daughter, Grace Winthrop Sears, who had recently married William Cabell Rives Jr., an attorney, who was a son of a United States senator from Virginia. The family remained in the house until it was sold in 1871, along with 42 Beacon, to the Somerset Club.

44 BEACON

This mostly original house was built by Harrison Gray Otis in 1833 for his daughter Sophia Harrison Otis and her husband, Andrew Ritchie. It was erected in what was originally part of the garden lot of 45 Beacon, located to the east of the main house. This part of the garden was the adjacent half to that which Otis sold to David Sears, who erected 43 Beacon there. In 1836, shortly after the houses' completion, Harrison Gray Otis's wife passed away, and Sophia and her husband moved into 45 Beacon to help care for her father.[86] Otis transferred ownership of the house to his son-in-law in 1837; Ritchie then rented it out.

One of the tenants was Francis Calley Gray, son of William Gray of Salem, one of the largest New England shipowners of his time, with a fleet of some sixty vessels.

Following Calley, the house was occupied by Samuel Austin, a merchant, who lived there until 1853, when he purchased 45 Beacon after the death of Harrison Gray Otis.

In 1853, Otis's son, James W., sold the house to the heirs of Robert Gould Shaw, a wealthy merchant and philanthropist. The heirs retained the house until 1874, when they sold to Alexander Cochrane, a chemical manufacturer and director of the American Bell Telephone Co.[87] from its beginning. He was also a trustee of the Museum of Fine Arts, to which he donated many works of art, including paintings by Stuart, Monet and Renoir.

In 1888, Cochrane sold the house to Ellen S. Dixey, wife of Richard Dixey, a concert pianist, who owned the property until 1925. Ellen Sturgis Tappan Dixey's family owned the Lenox estate called Tanglewood, which her family gave to the Boston Symphony Orchestra in 1936, creating a musical tradition that thrills music lovers every summer. The estate was named after Nathaniel Hawthorne's *Tanglewood Tales*.

In 1931, the house belonged to Elaine Sohier, who sold it in 1941 to Charles S. Bird, and in 1968 the ownership was transferred to the Somerset Club. Today, it is listed as a residential building comprising four to six family units.

45 Beacon

This grand mansion house was built in 1806 by Harrison Gray Otis on land included in the Copley estate purchase and allocated to Otis and Mason under the 1799 MVP Agreement of Partition.

This allotment, measuring 240 feet on Beacon Street, was divided in half, with Mason getting the western section (46, 47, 48 and 49 Beacon) and Otis getting the eastern half (43, 44 and 45 Beacon). The house was designed by Charles Bulfinch, nineteenth-century Boston's most famous architect, who had also designed Otis's previous two houses, first at 141 Cambridge Street (built in 1796) and then at 85 Mt. Vernon Street (built in 1801). He was also for a time a member of the MVP.

When 45 Beacon was originally built, it offered views of Boston Harbor and the Blue Hills to the south and west and was laid out with a garden to the east. Otis eventually decreased the property in size by selling the eastern half of the garden lot to David Sears. On the western half, he built a house that he gave to his daughter Sophia and her husband, Andrew Ritchie.

The house soon became the social center of Beacon Hill, where the Otises attracted many visiting dignitaries and hosted many gala events. While visiting Boston in 1831 during their historical tour of America, Alexis de Tocqueville and his traveling companion, Beaumont, attended a parade that was organized to assist the Poles in reuniting their partitioned country. Recounting their

Number 45 Beacon, the Harrison Gray Otis House, circa 1870, and 44 Beacon built on the original garden site. *Copyright © John F. Kennedy Library Foundation.*

observations of the parade, the Frenchmen commented, "Also in the procession had been the retiring Mayor of Boston, the last of the Federalist aristocrats, Mr. Harrison Gray Otis, who now invited them to his house." There they met his wife, Sally, and at once gained entrance to the circle around his daughter-in-law, Mrs. H.G. Otis Jr. "She was a rollicking, romping, good-humored woman, full of fun, and speaking French with great fluency and volubility."[88]

Typifying this social standing was a ball given by Otis in honor of President James Monroe upon his visit to Boston in 1817, an event described in detail in Eliza Quincy's *Memoir*. It was at this ball that President Monroe met with Charles Bulfinch, who was at the time selectman of the town of Boston. Monroe eventually appointed Bulfinch to finish the architectural work of the Capitol Building in Washington, D.C.

Otis was an inveterate politician starting with his election as a Federalist to the United States Congress, where he served from 1797 to 1801. In 1814, he served as a delegate to the Hartford Convention, which was called by the Federalists from Massachusetts and the other New England states in an effort to coordinate objections to the Jefferson and Madison Embargo Acts. They proposed a number of amendments and, interestingly, one—the presidential term limit—was finally approved in 1951.

Subsequently, Otis was elected a United States senator, serving from 1817 to 1822. He retired, however, almost a year before the end of his term, as he missed his family life in Boston and especially his wife, Sally, who was unable to accompany him to Washington for every session of the Senate. Following his senate career, Otis invested substantially in textile manufacturing and never strayed far from politics. He was elected the third mayor of Boston, serving from 1829 to 1831 and marking the end of his political life as an elected official.[89]

Otis lived in the house until his death in 1848, and shortly thereafter, in 1853, it was sold by his heirs to Samuel Austin, who was living at the time at 44 Beacon. Austin, who was a bachelor, "was so afraid that he or his friends might stumble at the top of the Bulfinch spiral staircase and roll down to the bottom that he replaced it by an ugly squarish one with broad landings."[90] Following the death of Samuel, his brother and business partner, Edward, remained living in the house. Edward, in memory of his deceased brother, gave Harvard College funds to erect a law building named Austin Hall, designed by H.H. Richardson.

After Austin's death in 1898, the house was sold to a relative, W. Austin Wadsworth, whose family used the home as a town house until 1929, when the property was transferred to New York congressman Lathrop Brown's wife, Helen Hooper Brown. In 1940, Mrs. Brown transferred the property to the Boston Council of the Boy Scouts of America as that organization's headquarters. The Boy Scouts retained the house until 1954, when the property then went to Miss Eleanora Sears as trustee for the Bulfinch House Trust, which was created by Ms. Sears and others to preserve the house for posterity. In 1958, the Bulfinch Trust transferred ownership to the American Meteorological Society, which had been renting space on Joy Street but outgrew it.[91] Today, the house still serves as the headquarters for the society.

46 BEACON

This large home was erected in 1914 by Eben D. Jordan, son of Eben Jordan, the founder of Boston's famous department store, Jordan Marsh & Co. It replaced both the home originally built here and 47 Beacon.

The original house was one of four similar residences, a quadruple row house constructed by builders Homer, Otis, Thaxter and Sprague in 1805 on land purchased in 1804 from Jonathan Mason.

In 1811, Daniel Pinckney Parker owned the house, and in 1816 he sold it to Thomas Cordis, a partner in Bellows, Cordis and Jones, importers of British dry goods. It was in 1816 that Parker purchased the Vinal land and

Numbers 49, 48 and 46 Beacon. The eleven-floor 48 Beacon was controversial, as it blocked residents' view of the statehouse's golden dome. Number 47 Beacon was absorbed into the expanded 46 Beacon.

began building 40 Beacon. Cordis retained the property until 1852, when he sold it to Henry A. Peirce, merchant. In the 1870s, Peirce was United States minister to the Kingdom of Hawaii under King Kalakaua. Peirce sold to Eben D. Jordan in 1866.

Jordan was one of the founders of the *Boston Globe* in 1872 and, along with Benjamin L. Marsh, was the co-founder of Jordan Marsh & Co., one of the first department stores in Boston. They pioneered the concept of consolidating wares in one place, saving the customer from having to go to a variety of different stores—hence departmentalized. Jordans, as it was commonly known, continued in business until it was acquired by Macy's Department Stores.

In 1913, Jordan purchased the adjacent house 47 Beacon, which had been totally changed from its original appearance, and proceeded, in 1914, to combine the two residences into a single palatial home constructed by McNeil Brothers, one of the foremost builders in early twentieth-century Boston.[92]

In 1924, the Jordan family sold the property to the Women's Republican Club of Massachusetts. Founded in 1921,[93] the club served as a meeting place for women where they could socialize and listen to concerts and lectures and where there were overnight accommodations. By the 1960s, however, it had moved from this grand residence, and ownership subsequently changed to the Boston Club, a private club with fifteen apartments, a dining room and fitness facilities, including a squash court. By the 1960s, the club was offering hotel accommodations and was a public restaurant.

In 1977, the building was purchased by the Unification Church of Massachusetts, which owns the building today and uses it primarily for conferences.

47 BEACON

This site was the location of one of four similar residences built on land sold by MVP member Jonathan Mason in 1804 to John Osborn.

The house was constructed by builders Homer, Otis, Thaxter and Sprague and sold in 1810 to John McLean. His widow, Susan, received title to the property through her husband's will and then sold it in 1829 to heirs of John Lowell.

Created by John Lowell Jr., the Lowell Trust, later known as the Lowell Institute, continues today providing lectures for "the intelligence and information of [New England's] inhabitants."[94] The trust rented the home

Numbers 49, 48 and 47 Beacon, circa 1865. Along with 46 Beacon, these were built on speculation in 1805. *Courtesy of the Bostonian Society/Old State House Museum.*

Numbers 49, 48, 47 and 46 Beacon, circa 1870. Number 46 Beacon retains much of its original size and window locations, while 47 and 48 Beacon have been replaced. Number 49 Beacon has been greatly modified. *Courtesy of Historic New England.*

to various tenants, including Theodore Chase, who lived there until 1840, when the Lowell trust sold the property.

In 1845, the house was purchased by Martin Brimmer, who rented it out until it was razed in 1869. He then erected two houses that covered the site:

47 Beacon, where Brimmer was to reside, and 48 Beacon, which was to be rented and had been in the Brimmer family since 1812.

These ornate buildings were designed by famed architect Richard Morris Hunt in 1869–70. Hunt later designed the Vanderbilt estate Biltmore in Asheville, North Carolina, and the pedestal for the Statute of Liberty in New York Harbor. Hunt was a personal friend of Brimmer's,[95] who often visited Hunt in New York, where most of his work was done. Brimmer, son of the Boston mayor of the same name, was both a philanthropic and civic-minded citizen who was, among other things, a trustee of the Boston Athenaeum, president of the Museum of Fine Arts and one of the founders of the Union Club.

In 1906, his widow, Marianne Brimmer, sold the residence to Marie T. Garland, and in 1913 James A. Garland sold to Eben D. Jordan, who incorporated the building, along with 46 Beacon, into his new lavish home, thus eliminating Hunt's façade and the 47 Beacon address.

48 BEACON

This controversial twelve-story apartment house was built on the site of the original house that was one of four similar residences built on land sold by MVP Jonathan Mason.

Constructed by Homer, Otis, Thaxter and Sprague, the dwelling was sold to Andrew Brimmer in 1812. Brimmer rented the house to tenants until 1835, when it was occupied by Martin Brimmer. In 1850, it was owned by Martin, who rebuilt it in 1869, along with 47 Beacon, as a double row house designed by Richard Morris Hunt.

When the new houses designed by Hunt were erected, the dimensions were changed from their identical footprints and frontage on Beacon Street. This house changed its frontage of thirty feet to twenty-two feet but was not visibly smaller, as the Hunt design blended the two addresses. The only noticeable difference was that this house was four stories while 47 Beacon was three.

Following the demise of Brimmer, the estate sold the house, in 1879, to Louise H. Williams. Williams in turn sold the property, in 1896, to W. French, who in 1903 transferred ownership to Robert H. Gardiner, Richard C. Storey and himself as trustees for the 48 Beacon Street Trust.

The grand Hunt house was then razed, and in 1913 the trust proceeded to erect the existing twelve-story apartment building. The height of this new building was restricted by Massachusetts legislative acts that were promulgated to protect the visibility of the statehouse dome and retain the character of the settled areas of Beacon Hill. They were the first of their kind in the United States.

The building exists today as condominium residences with nineteen units.

49 BEACON

This house replaced the one originally built here as one of the four similar residences constructed by Homer, Otis, Thaxter and Sprague. It was described by Allen Chamberlain, in his 1925 book *Beacon Hill*, as "the only vestige remaining of these buildings...part of the brick walls."[96] The dwelling was sold to Elizabeth Sumner in 1806 and in 1815 to General William H. Sumner. He had been the owner of Noddles Island, which he developed into the East Boston Company, which in turn administered the commercial and residential growth of East Boston.[97]

In 1820, the house was purchased by Peter Parker, merchant, and as late as 1870, J. Harleston Parker[98] was the owner.

This Parker was an architect who studied at MIT and the École des Beaux Arts in Paris. In 1921, he established, in memory of his father, the Harleston Parker Medal to recognize "the most beautiful piece of architectural building, monument or structure within the city limits of Boston or by the Metropolitan Parks District." The medal is awarded annually by the Boston Society of Architects.[99] In 1882, Parker sold the house, and in 1899 William Lowell Putnam owned it.

William Lowell Putnam was the brother-in-law of Percival Lowell, an astronomer and an attorney and partner in the firm of Putnam, Putnam and Bell. He was deeply involved with the Lowell Observatory and was responsible for investing Percival's estate for the benefit of the observatory. Putnam died in 1924, and his widow, Elizabeth, established a college-level mathematics competition, the William Lowell Putnam Mathematical Competition, which exists to this day.[100]

The major change to the façade of the building from 1870 to the present was the relocation of the front entrance from the first floor to the ground floor; the older entrance area is now used as a sitting area with a large window overlooking the Boston Common.

In 1936, the William Lowell and Elizabeth B. Putnam estate sold the house, and today the building is condominiums.

11

Spruce Street to Charles Street

50 Beacon

This full-block building replaced the original house that was erected here in 1805 by Samuel Alleyne Otis, brother of the Patriot James Otis and father of Harrison Gray Otis. The dwelling was constructed on the easterly half of a fifty-foot parcel of land on Beacon Street that S.A. Otis purchased from the Mount Vernon Proprietors (MVP) in 1804.

Samuel A. Otis was a mercantile businessman whose company was appointed, in 1777, as supplier of clothing for the Continental army. He was a delegate to the Continental Congress in 1787, and when the new federal government was set up shortly thereafter, he was appointed, through the efforts of Vice President John Adams, to the post of secretary of the United States Senate, a position he retained until his death in 1814. He was one of the original directors of the Massachusetts Bank, founded in 1784.

He married Elizabeth Gray, the daughter of Harrison Gray, a prominent Tory who left Boston during the British evacuation of 1776 and settled in London. This Gray had been the provincial treasurer and was considered one of the most notorious conspirators of the British Loyalists. He was banished forever from the United States. Samuel Otis's second wife, Mary Smith Gray Otis, was a cousin of Abigail Smith Adams, wife of President John Adams. After the death of Samuel, Mary continued living in this house with their two daughters, Harriet and Mary.[101] Mary was treasurer of the Boston Female Asylum and was the last Otis resident. She sold the house in 1872 to Charles Amory.

Numbers 51 and 50 Beacon.

Numbers 53, 52, 51 and 50 Beacon, circa 1870. Numbers 52 and 50 Beacon have been changed completely, while 53 and 51 Beacon remain the same. *Courtesy of the Bostonian Society/Old State House Museum.*

Amory retained ownership until 1889, when his estate sold to the trustees of the Puritan Club, who in 1890 erected a new building that was to be their home. This new building extended along Spruce Street from Beacon to Branch Streets, with the main entrance relocated to Spruce Street.

The Puritan Club, founded in 1884, was an all-purpose club with the unusual feature for the times of a ladies' dining room and, "as far as one can gather, filled a need that was not a whit different from the Somerset Club, half a block up the street, and the Union, not much further away."[102] The club remained popular until just before World War I, when membership in city clubs decreased due in large part to the suburban exodus. By 1915, the club had moved from the building, and it was occupied by the Allyn and Bacon Publishing Co.

The property was sold in 1927 to Viola D. Fuller, wife of Alvan T. Fuller, governor of Massachusetts from 1925 to 1929 and United States congressman from 1917 to 1921. In 1955, the building was sold by Viola Fuller and was later converted to offices.

Today, the building houses condominium residences.

This location is considered by many to be the homesite of the original settler William Blackstone, and honoring this, there is attached to the face of this building a tablet that reads:

Reverend William Blaxton
Born Horncastle Parish Lincolnshire England
5 March 1596
Graduate of Emanuel College England 1621
First Settler of Shawmut 1625
Near here stood his dwelling
He removed to Rhode Island in 1635
Where he died May 26, 1675
The place of his seclusion
Became the seat of a great city

Placed by the City of Boston 1924
The tablet restored by Gilbert Henderson Foundation

51 Beacon

The site on which this four-story house was erected was the westerly half of the land purchased in 1804 by Samuel Alleyne Otis from the MVP and sold the following year to Peter Osgood, housewright, and Jeremiah

Gardner. They constructed the house and in 1806 sold it to John Rose Greene. In 1809, it was owned by David Sears Sr., who in 1823 sold to Fifty Associates.

Fifty Associates rented the house to various tenants. In 1856, it sold the house to Frederick R. Sears, and as late as 1915, the property belonged to Albertine Sears.

In 1950, the house belonged to Edythe Gilman, who still owned it in 1953.

Today, the building, which appears much as it did in 1870, is divided into five condominium residences.

52 BEACON

This much-altered house was constructed on land that was originally part of the Copley estate and was owned by Harrison Gray Otis in 1804. Otis then sold the parcel, and in 1806 it was owned by Thomas Kendall, a tailor and real estate developer, who divided the land into halves and then had a house built on each lot, probably by Otis, Thaxter et al.

In 1832, the house was owned by T.H. Carter of T.H. Carter & Co., which produced stereotypes and published children's magazines. Carter then sold it in 1834 to D.P. Parker.

Parker rented the property for a time to Edmund Quincy, who was married to Parker's daughter, Lucilla. Edmund Quincy was an abolitionist and author and edited publications such as the *Anti-Slavery Standard* and the *Abolitionist*. In 1864, the owner was Henry J. Bigelow, physician. Bigelow was a surgeon at Massachusetts General Hospital and wrote many papers, including one about Dr. William Thomas Green Morton's first use of ether in a surgical operation performed by Dr. Joseph Warren Collins.

After several owners, the house became the property of Provident Institute for Savings, and in 1936 that company sold it to the Fay School. M. Irene Fay owned it as late as 1953.

Current use is both residential and commercial.

53 BEACON

The original house here was probably built by the firm of Otis, Thaxter et al. on vacant land purchased by Kendall in 1806 and divided into two lots. Kendall sold this western house in 1809 to William Gill of Philadelphia.

In 1816, Gill sold to Samuel Appleton, who lived here until completing, in 1820, his house at 37 Beacon Street. Appleton then used this house as rental property, with various tenants including Isaac Bangs.

Following Samuel Appleton's death in 1853, his widow, Mary, left the mansion at 37 Beacon and moved here following substantial modifications to the house. It was described by her niece, Fanny, wife of poet Henry Wadsworth Longfellow, as a "little birdcage of a house." It curved outward toward the street, all bow window in shape but only two narrow windows wide. The front door had a grille with the initials "S.A." on it. The ground floor was granite and the upper floors brownstone. It rose higher than William Appleton's (54 Beacon) delicately balustraded roof next door—and there it still stands.[103]

Numbers 55, 54, 53 and 52 Beacon. Numbers 55 and 54 Beacon, built in 1806, are mirror-image row houses.

After several owners, the Samuel Hooper estate sold the house in 1890 to Mary and Harriet Walker.

The Walker sisters had inherited from their uncle, Theophilus Wheeler Walker, Gore Place in Waltham, Massachusetts. Gore Place was built in 1806 as a summer residence for Rebecca and Christopher Gore, a former Massachusetts governor and United States senator.

Following the example of their uncle's generosity to Bowdoin College, the sisters donated funds to erect an art museum in his memory, the Walker Art Building, designed by McKim, Mead and White, the New York architectural firm that also designed the Boston Public Library.

As reported by news accounts in 1904, the sisters also left to St. Paul's Church more than $1 million "for the purpose of building, establishing, and maintaining a cathedral or Bishop's Church of the Protestant Episcopal Church in the City of Boston."[104]

Mary S. and Harriet S. Walker's estate sold the house in 1907. In 1910, L.C. Page and Co., publisher, was the owner.

The Page Company still owned it in 1953, and subsequently the building was used for business purposes and law offices, housing at one time Swartz & Swartz, internationally known product liability attorneys.

Today, the building is residential condominiums.

54 BEACON

This mostly original house was erected on land that was allocated to Jonathan Mason by the MVP Division of Lands of 1806. Mason sold the land in 1806 to James Smith Colburn, who divided the parcel into two equal lots, 54 and 55 Beacon, upon which he built, the same year, a brick double row house. The design of these houses is attributed to Asher Benjamin.

Colburn sold the easterly house in 1808 to Nathan Appleton, who lived there until he built a new and larger house, to which he moved in 1819. After building his new house, he sold this house in 1820 to his first cousin, William Appleton.

William started in the shipping business with his cousins Samuel and Nathan Appleton and soon became a businessman in his own right as a successful shipbuilder, shipowner and merchant. He later served as a United States congressman from 1851 to 1855 and again in 1861. In 1860, prior to the start of the Civil War hostilities, he dined with President Lincoln, whom he found "cheerful and talked freely of the State of Affairs."[105] The following year, when returning to Congress by sea, he was aboard a ship awaiting the tide to enter Charleston Harbor the night the shelling of Fort Sumter occurred, and upon arrival at the port, he was one of twelve who inspected the damage.[106]

In 1862, William transferred ownership to his son, Charles Hook Appleton, and in 1913, the house was owned by George von Lengerke Meyer.[107] (Meyer's wife, Marian Alice Appleton, was the daughter of Charles Hook Appleton and Isabella Mason). Meyer was ambassador to Italy and Russia under President T. Roosevelt, and when serving in Russia he arranged for the peace conference in Portsmouth, New Hampshire, between Japan and Russia. He was later appointed secretary of the navy under President William Howard Taft. Mrs. George von Lengerke Meyer gave the J.S. Copley painting *Watson and the Shark* to the Museum of Fine Arts in Boston.[108]

In 1942, the house was divided into two parts: lot A and lot D. Lot A was the main house, 54 Beacon, fronting on Beacon Street, while the rear of the house, lot D, was 33 Branch Street.

Today, the property is listed as an apartment building.

55 BEACON

This original house was built on the western half of the lot allocated to Jonathan Mason and sold to James Smith Colburn, a merchant, in 1806. Colburn lived in 55 Beacon from 1807 until 1819, when it was sold to Samuel Ward, who rented the house to various people. In 1833, Ward sold it to Augustus Thorndike of Newport, Rhode Island. Thorndike, a benefactor of the arts, assisted with the first attempt for an art gallery in Boston when the Boston Athenaeum opened a room to artists that contained a collection of casts—a gift from Thorndike.

In 1845, Thorndike sold the house to William Hickling Prescott, historian and author, who wrote *History of the Reign of Ferdinand and Isabella, History of Peru* and *The Conquest of Mexico*. He was a member of the famed Saturday Club, a dining club whose membership included such notables as Henry Wadsworth Longfellow, Nathaniel Hawthorne, Oliver Wendell Holmes and Richard Henry Dana. Upon his death in 1859, Prescott had one of the largest private libraries in Boston. He was the grandson of Colonel William Prescott, who led the Minutemen during the 1775 Battle of Bunker Hill.

The estate kept the house until 1872, when it was sold to Franklin Gordon Dexter, attorney, who had married Hattie Appleton, daughter of William Appleton, owner of 54 Beacon. Dexter, who was in the shipping business with his father-in-law, also was the founder of the Temperance Society in Boston.

Dexter and the Appletons decided to divide the houses into two lots each. This house, 55 Beacon, was divided into lot B, the front section of the house facing Beacon Street, and lot C, the rear section facing Branch Street. In 1942, the properties were sold, and in 1944, the Massachusetts Society of Colonial Dames of America owned lot B.

Today, the society owns the property as a museum and opens its doors frequently to the general public for tours.

56 BEACON

This mostly original house was erected on the eastern half of lot 4A, allocated to Harrison Gray Otis by the MVP 1806 Division of Lands.

Otis sold the entire parcel, comprising 56 and 57 Beacon, in 1819 to Ephraim Marsh, builder and architect. Marsh then divided the land into two equal lots, upon which he built a brick double row house. This easterly dwelling was sold in 1820 to William H. Eliot, builder of the Tremont House Hotel.

Following Eliot's death, his estate sold the house, in 1831, to the estate of Georgina Lowell. It was occupied by her husband, John Lowell Jr., founder of the Lowell Institute Lectures, a lecture series that offered "free public lectures in religion, science and the arts."[109] The lectures are still given to this day.

John Jr. died in Bombay in 1836, and the property stayed in the family until 1875, with Guy Lowell born here in 1870. Guy studied architecture at the École des Beaux-Arts in Paris and was the architect of the Fenway entrance to the Museum of Fine Arts, as well as the hexagonal courthouse in New York City.

Numbers 61, 60, 59, 58, 57 and 56 Beacon. Built in 1820, 57 and 56 Beacon resemble the classic design of their neighbors, 55 and 54 Beacon.

In 1875, the Lowell family sold the house to F. Gordon Dexter. In 1894, Dexter sold it to Williams S. Bigelow, whose family still owned it in 1927. The estate sold the property in 1927 to Francis Bacon Lothrop, and in 1953 it belonged to Eleanor Lothrop.

Today, the property is listed as a single-family residence.

57 BEACON

This mostly original house was built on the western half of the lot that had been allocated to Harrison Gray Otis. The entire parcel was sold by Otis in 1819 to Ephraim Marsh, who sold this house in 1820 to David Eckley, son of the Reverend Joseph Eckley of the Old South Church.

On July 7, 1824, a conflagration known at the time as the Beacon Street Fire broke out in the passageway (which still exists today) to the west of 64 Beacon, a house being built by John Bryant, and quickly ignited the wooden outbuildings to the rear of his house. The fire spread rapidly and consumed seven brick dwellings (58–64 Beacon) while sparing Eckley's house, his being the one at which the fire was finally stopped.[110]

Numbers 61 (partially shown), 60, 59, 58 and 57 Beacon, circa 1870. *Courtesy of the Bostonian Society/Old State House Museum.*

The house remained in the Eckley family until 1882, when it was sold to George Nixon Black, an avid art collector and benefactor to the Museum of Fine Arts.

A native of Maine, he left the Nixon family home, Woodlawn, with its extensive gardens, to Hancock County as a museum. His family retained ownership of 57 Beacon until 1952, when the George N. Black estate willed a portion to the Museum of Fine Arts.

Today, the building is residential condominiums.

58 BEACON

This house was built on the eastern third of lot 3A allocated to General Henry Jackson as trustee for Hepzibah C. Swan by the MVP 1806 Division of Lands. Jackson sold to architect and builder Asher Benjamin in 1807. Benjamin, who was originally a carpenter, wrote *The American Builder's Companion*, which was to become a handbook for many housewrights in the early nineteenth century. Benjamin erected this house and sold it to Stephen Bean, attorney, in 1808. The house was destroyed in the fire of 1824 and was immediately rebuilt in 1825.

Bean sold the house shortly thereafter. In 1829, Elisha Parks was the owner and rented out the premises to Elbridge Gerry, surveyor. In 1850, Christopher Chadwick of Chadwick Dry Goods owned it and then sold, in 1862, to John A. Blanchard, merchant in the dry goods business of Blanchard, Converse & Co.

In 1874, the John Blanchard estate sold to Cora Lyman Shaw, who transferred the house in 1919 to Amy Shaw Warren, wife of Dr. John Collins Warren, a professor of surgery in the Harvard Medical School[111] and descendant of General Joseph Warren of Bunker Hill fame. In 1952, Geraldine S. Hanley was the owner. Hanley purchased 57 Beacon the same year.

Today, the building is residential condominiums.

59 BEACON

This slender building was erected on the center third of lot 3A allocated to General Henry Jackson as trustee for Hepzibah C. Swan. Jackson sold this parcel in 1808 to Daniel Tuttle, a bricklayer, who erected a house that was destroyed in the Beacon Street Fire of 1824. Tuttle rebuilt the house and then sold it to William Appleton in 1825. Appleton kept the building for only one year and then sold it to David Sears II in 1826.

Sears leased the house to various tenants, including merchants Ozias Goodwin and, later, Theodore Rich. In 1857, Sears sold the house, and in 1859 the owner was J.T.W. Sargent, who was married to Amelia Jackson Holmes. Her brother was Oliver Wendell Holmes Jr., who was to become an associate justice of the United States Supreme Court for thirty years (1902–32). He was listed as trustee for the Sargent estate in 1898, and in 1924 Holmes, as trustee under the will of Amelia J. Sargent, sold the house to Horace Chapin, who also owned 60 Beacon.

In the 1920s, the building was the location of the Boston Antique Shop: "Things you don't see every day—A miniature museum of New England antique rarities on exhibition and for sale."[112]

Chapin's sister, Margaret Osgood, received title to the property (along with 60 Beacon) under the will of Chapin, and in 1943 the house belonged to Alfred F. Doyle, who owned it as late as 1953.

Today, the building is listed as residential and commercial.

60 BEACON

This narrow house was erected on the western third of lot 3A allocated to General Henry Jackson and was sold by him to John Cotton, painter, in 1807. Cotton then constructed a brick house on the site, which he was renting out when it was destroyed in the Beacon Street Fire of 1824. In 1830, Cotton rented the rebuilt house to Samuel Austin, a shipping merchant who, with his brother Edward, started the first transatlantic Boston–Liverpool line with three packets, the *Topaz, Amethyst* and *Emerald*. The Austin brothers later lived at 45 Beacon.

In 1835, Cotton sold the house to Samuel Austin Jr., and in 1877 the dwelling belonged to Henry J. Bigelow. In 1880, Henry's son, Dr. William Sturgis Bigelow, an instructor in surgery at the Harvard Medical School and long associated with Massachusetts General Hospital, was the owner and was living in the house. Bigelow also lived in Japan for a time and studied Buddhism, on which subject he published a book entitled *Buddhism and Immortality*. In 1908, he sold the house, and Horace C. Chapin kept the property until 1940. In 1946, the house was owned by Ronald T. Lyman Jr. until as late as 1953.

Today, the building is a residential two-family property.

61 BEACON

This house was constructed on the easterly half of lot 2A allocated to Benjamin Joy by the MVP 1806 Division of Lands. Benjamin, younger brother of Dr. John Joy, sold this land in 1808 to Jeremiah Gardner, housewright, who in turn sold the land in 1812 to John Howe.

Howe divided the property into two lots and in 1817 sold this easterly portion to William Minot, attorney, who built the house with the design attributed to Peter Banner, architect of the Park Street Church.

The house was destroyed in the Beacon Street Fire of 1824 and subsequently rebuilt. It remained in the Minot family for many years, and in 1874 George R. Minot sold the property to Elizabeth B. Bryant. Bryant's estate retained ownership until 1917, and in 1927 the house belonged to Christian A. Herter.

Herter served as a United States congressman from 1943 to 1953 and then was governor of Massachusetts from 1953 to 1957. He was later United States secretary of state from 1959 to 1961 under President Eisenhower. In 1947, Christian A. Herter sold the house to Constance J. Whiting, who still owned it in 1953.

This building has been described by some as "Beacon Hill's pride" because of its very elegant façade. Today, it houses residential condominiums.

62 BEACON

The house originally here was constructed on the westerly half of lot 2A, which John Howe sold in 1819 to builder Ephraim Marsh, who proceeded that same year to build a house that he sold to Charlotte Rice, wife of Samuel B. Rice. This house was erected partially on the solid land of Beacon Hill and partially on filled land that was originally the shoreline of the Charles River Basin mud flats. In order to expand the available land for development, the MVP proceeded to fill in recently acquired Copley Estate lands "toward the water."

According to Carleton's map of circa 1803, the distance from Walnut Street to the edge of the beach measured 850 feet, composing the western boundary of Copley's estate along Beacon Street

The house was destroyed in the Beacon Street Fire of 1824 and was rebuilt in 1825. In 1826, the property was transferred to Henry G. Rice, merchant and importer of British goods.

Numbers 64, 63 and 62 (partially shown) Beacon, circa 1870.

In 1853, the Rice estate sold to Benjamin F. Burgess, a commission merchant with the firm of B.F. Burgess & Sons. In 1884, the house was sold, due to Burgess's insolvency, to James C. Jordan, trustee for Eben Jordan, and then the property was transferred, in 1888, by the trust to James C. Jordan himself.

In 1900, the property was auctioned to William S. Bryant, and in 1920 it was sold to Henry D. Tudor and Gerald G.E. Street, trustees of the 62 Beacon Street Real Estate Trust, which razed the 1825 house and erected a new building running the full depth of the lot from Beacon Street to Branch Street.

Numbers 66 (the "Bachelor Apartments"), 64, 63 and 62 Beacon. Number 62 Beacon was replaced in 1920 by a new house, while 64 and 63 Beacon remain unaltered.

In 1953, the owners were Caleb W. Warner and Mary Cabot Briggs. Today, the building is classified as residential, with four to six family units.

63 BEACON

This house was erected on the eastern portion of lot 1A, which had been allocated to Jonathan Mason by the MVP 1806 Division of Lands. In 1820, Mason sold this large lot to Ephraim Marsh, who divided the lot into two parcels.

The lot was created by filling the site with gravel, which the MVP had taken from Mt. Vernon. The easterly corner of this house, according to Gleaner, was the point where the sea reached, as "Mr. Bryant informs me, that when he dug his cellar he came to the natural beach, with its rounded pebble stones, at the depth of three to four feet below the surface."[113]

On this easterly parcel, Marsh built a house and sold it to Elizabeth Coolidge in 1821. Coolidge married Tasker H. Swett, merchant, that same year. The house, which was destroyed in the Beacon Street Fire of 1824 and was subsequently rebuilt, stayed in the Swett family until 1910, when the William B. Swett estate sold to Frances C. Sturgis.

In 1940, Frances C. Sturgis sold the house to L. Vernon Briggs, a renowned psychologist and director of the Massachusetts Department of Mental Hygiene, who also owned 64 Beacon, where he resided. In 1953, the house was owned by Lloyd Cabot Briggs, a noted anthropologist.

Today, the property is part of the King's Chapel House.

64 BEACON

This house replaced the original one that was constructed completely on filled land in the western section of lot 1A, allocated to Harrison Gray Otis in 1806. Otis sold the land in 1806 to Nathaniel Call, housewright, and Call sold the parcel in 1810 to developer Uriah Cotting, creator of the Mill Dam later known as Western Avenue and then Beacon Street.

In 1814, Cotting sold to John Bryant, and in the same year Bryant was assessed for "an unfinished house." Bryant was a partner with William Sturgis in the China trade firm of Bryant and Sturgis and as early as the 1840s[114] invested in railroads outside of Massachusetts.

In July 1824, just as Bryant's house was being completed, a fire started in a nearby carpenter's shop causing a conflagration that consumed not only Bryant's house but also seven houses east of Bryant's; the fire was finally checked at 57 Beacon.

> *Mr. Bryant had the advantage over his neighbors of not being incommoded by any furniture or family, as he had not yet taken possession...It should never be forgotten that it was solely owing to the existence of this open space [Boston Common] on this occasion that the entire southern portion of our city was not destroyed. The range of trees at the foot of the Beacon Street Mall rendered a truly important service. Suffering the flames of martyrdom, they died at their post of duty.*[115]

The house was then rebuilt and remained in the Bryant family through 1900, when the Bryant Real Estate Trust sold the property in 1908 to Dr. Lloyd Vernon Briggs, and in 1953 it was still owned by the family. In 1903, Briggs had coordinated the effort to save the Park Street Church from sale by its membership and subsequent demolition by a group that wanted to replace it with a commercial structure.[116] His efforts were successful, as the church stands today as a victory for early architectural preservationists.

Conservation efforts are also apparent in this house, as the front parlor on the second floor retains the original early nineteenth-century wallpaper made by Zuber of France, and in addition, the house has some purple panes of glass in the front windows visible from the street. These panes, original to the house, are a result of sunlight bringing out an imperfection in the glass, which originally came from Hamburg, Germany, and was installed in some houses built in the 1820s.

Today this historic home is the King's Chapel Parish House.

65 BEACON

This seven-story building designed by acclaimed architects McKim, Mead and White was constructed in 1889 and replaced an 1824 double house.

The first building erected here was built on filled land created in 1803 by the MVP as part of its project of making land from the shoreline (then at

Numbers 69 and 66 Beacon. The triple row house of 69, 68 and 67 Beacon was replaced by the new 69 Beacon.

Numbers 66 and 65 Beacon, circa 1870. These were replaced by the "Bachelor Apartments." *Copyright © John F. Kennedy Library Foundation.*

62 Beacon Street) to the west, including the creation of a new road named Charles Street recognized by the town in 1805. On the northeast corner of Charles and Beacon Streets, the MVP created six lots running northerly from Beacon and along Charles Street. It sold the corner lot in 1805 to John Woodbury, who erected a building as early as 1814. This building was probably destroyed in the Beacon Hill fire of 1824 and rebuilt as early as 1825 as a double house, later 65 and 66 Beacon.

In 1835, the property was sold to George H. Kuhn, and the Kuhn family retained the building until 1887. In 1889, T. Quincy Browne and J. Morris Meredith were the owners, and they proceeded to remove the existing houses, replacing them with a residential seven-story building dubbed the "Bachelor Apartments."

Browne and Meredith sold the new building in 1898 to Suffolk Real Estate Trust. In 1925, it was sold to Mary C. Briggs, who still owned it in 1938.

Today, the property is both residential and commercial.

66 BEACON

This was the western portion of the building that housed 65 and 66 Beacon, with 66 Beacon facing Charles Street. Its address is sometimes listed as being on Charles Street. This house derived from the same owner lineage as 65 Beacon. It was also demolished in 1890 and replaced by the "Bachelor Apartments," which today uses 66 Beacon as its address.

CHARLES STREET TO RIVER STREET

THE PUBLIC GARDEN

To walk through Boston's much-loved Public Garden paths and enjoy its beauty at any time of year is to reunite with the thoughts and love of nature that inspired the founders of the park that we see today.

Until Charles Street was laid out in 1803, the Common ended at the Charles River Basin's edge. In this marshy area, including Fox Hill, a number of ropewalks were erected that had previously been located on Pearl Street. Following a devastating fire in 1794, the Town of Boston wanted no more highly flammable buildings in the town center. To encourage this policy, the town gave the rope makers title to the marshy area beyond the Common on which to erect their buildings.

These ropewalks, which stretched some eleven hundred feet along the marsh, burned down in their new location in 1806, and although they were rebuilt many times, they were totally destroyed in 1823.

It was after the creation of Charles Street in 1803, the subsequent filling in of the flats along Beacon Street by the MVP and the opening of the Mill Dam Road (later extending Beacon Street) that the ropewalk lands became of use and therefore of value.

Ironically, the city was required to purchase the lands from the rope makers for $55,000—which it had given to them for free not many years before—and it was this acquisition that allowed the city to set aside the land for the Public Garden.

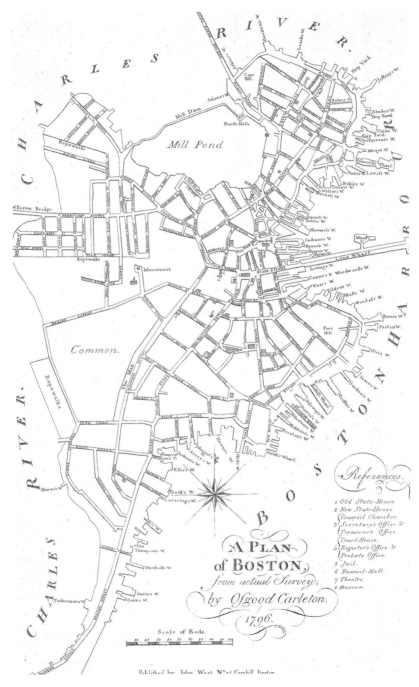

This Carleton map of 1796 shows the ropewalks area to the west of Boston Common. It became the Public Garden in 1837.

The Public Garden in the foreground, circa 1850, looking east toward Boston Harbor.

In 1824, a vote was passed denying the city's right to sell the land and requiring it to keep the space "open for circulation of air from the west for the sake of the health of the citizens."[117]

The area was not immediately used for a garden, but in 1837 a petition was presented to the city to establish a botanical garden. The city complied by leasing twenty acres to a group headed by Horace Gray, a successful manufacturer of iron.[118] This group created a large conservatory divided into four galleries for both plants and birds. Located near the corner of Beacon and Charles Streets, the conservatory was very popular with the public until the building was destroyed by fire. By 1847, the patron, Horace Gray, had lost his fortune, and the garden went into decline.

By 1852, the city had reacquired the land with the intention of dividing the area into house lots. However, due to controversy among the city, state and the Boston & Roxbury Mill Corporation over land rights, the disposition of the area remained undecided until 1856, when the state legislature ruled in the Back Bay (or Public Garden) Act that no building other than a city hall could ever be erected on the land, "except as are expedient for horticultural purposes."[119]

Today, the original area, plus an additional two acres along Arlington Street, composes the Boston Public Garden. The lagoon, with its swan boats and bridge, and many statues and fountains highlighted by Ball's George Washington create what Bostonians and visitors alike consider to be "a public pride."[120]

BOSTON & ROXBURY MILL CORPORATION

The Boston & Roxbury Mill Corporation, headed by Uriah Cotting and Isaac P. Davis, was granted a charter by the General Court of Massachusetts in 1814. The corporation was authorized to build a dam from the intersection of Beacon Street and Charles Street, running west to Sewall's Point in Brookline, and also to erect a cross dam from Gravelly's Point in Brookline to the main dam.[121]

The cross dam divided the basin into two parts: the full basin, into which the Charles River waters would flow on incoming tides, and the receiving basin, into which the water from the full basin would flow at low tide. The releasing of the water would operate the mills, which were designed to produce flour and iron and were located on top of the dam. The Town of Boston also authorized the corporation to erect a toll road on top of the dam to provide a much-shortened route from Boston to Brookline. This toll road, first named the Mill Dam Road, then Western Avenue and finally Beacon

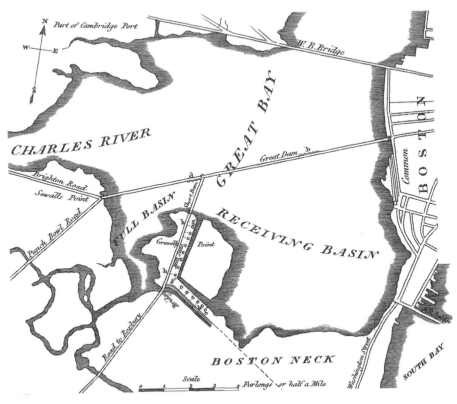

Hales map of 1821, showing the layout of the "great dam," which became Beacon Street.

Panoramic photograph looking westward taken from the cupola of the Massachusetts Statehouse in 1858, showing the Charles River Basin and, in the upper right, the Mill Dam Road, later Beacon Street. *Courtesy of Boston Athenaeum.*

Street, first opened to traffic in 1821 and still exists under today's Beacon Street. It proved to be the only part of the dam project that was successful.

In 1824, the Boston & Roxbury Mill Corporation petitioned the Massachusetts legislature for rights to the land north of the dam and was granted the right to "use and occupy any part of the vacant flats lying on the north side of their dam, and west of the low water mark…and within two hundred feet of said dam, and fill any part thereof, and put sheds and buildings on same." It also petitioned the city for approval to erect buildings over the flats east of the sluiceways. This low-water mark ended at what is now 87 Beacon Street, and all properties east of 87 Beacon belonged to the MVP, while property from 87 Beacon west belonged to the Boston & Roxbury Mill Corporation. Thus, as a result of this act, the corporation was able to fill the land and sell the same at its discretion. In the same year, it gave the MVP permission to utilize the dam (and road) as a southerly wall for its project of filling in the flats and erecting buildings thereupon.

This series of events, while not considered in the original plans of the Mill Dam, created the ability to fill in the land, including the flats of Beacon Hill and the entire Back Bay. This increased the size and importance of Boston immeasurably, so it is easy to understand why Nathaniel I. Bowditch called Uriah Cotting the "Chief Benefactor of Boston."[122]

67 BEACON

The building originally erected here was placed on filled land that was created by the Mount Vernon Proprietors (MVP) between the years 1803 and 1805. This land at the northwest corner of what is now Beacon and

Numbers 69, 68 and 67 Beacon, circa 1870. *Copyright © John F. Kennedy Library Foundation.*

Charles Streets was sold in 1804 by Harrison Gray Otis to Joseph Batson and Daniel Maynard, and in 1817 Elisha Penniman was the owner. In 1843, Penniman sold the land and buildings to George M. Dexter, developer and builder, who divided the land into three lots and constructed three connected row houses, 67, 68 and 69 Beacon, all of which faced Beacon Street.

In 1844, 67 Beacon was owned by George Gardner, and the property remained in the Gardner family as late as 1916, when the trustees under Gardner's will sold it. In 1917, the building was owned by the Beacon Street Apartment Trust, which also purchased at the same time 68 and 69 Beacon. All three houses were subsequently razed to make way for the 1917 construction of the present nine-floor building on the site.

In 1918, a new trust was formed, the 68 Beacon Street Trust, and in 1922 the new building was sold to William Randolph Hearst, who retained the property for four years.

In 1945, the building was owned by 68 Beacon Street, Inc., and had sixteen apartments, each with seven to eight rooms and two baths. Today, the building is cooperative residences.

Looking westward from Charles Street, circa 1870. *Courtesy of the Bostonian Society/Old State House Museum.*

68 BEACON

The dwelling house originally constructed on this site was one of three row houses built by George M. Dexter, who sold the land in 1843 to Edward S. Rand, attorney, while the house itself was completed in 1845. Rand rented the house to various tenants, including James Read, who moved to 90 Beacon in 1853. That year, Rand was occupying the house himself.

In 1871, Rand sold the house to J. Ingersoll Bowditch and Mary Lowell Putnam, trustees under the will of Samuel R. Putnam. In 1914, C.P. Bowditch owned the house, and in 1917, the property was owned by the Beacon Street Apartment Trust. The house was then razed, along with 67 and 69 Beacon, to make way for the new building that exists today.

69 BEACON

The house originally erected here was one of three similar dwellings erected by developer and architect George M. Dexter and sold in 1844 to Charles H. Mills, who was in the dry goods business.

In 1847, Mills sold an interest in the property to Edmond D. Dwight, and in 1850 Dwight and Mills were renting the house to William W. Tucker of the commission merchant house of Upham, Tucker & Co. In 1853, they sold the property to Tucker, and in 1861 Tucker sold to Charles C. Chadwick, who moved to this address from 58 Beacon.

Chadwick retained the property until 1915, and in 1917 it belonged to the Beacon Street Apartment Trust, which then razed the house, along with 67 and 68 Beacon, replacing it with the building that we see today. This number is presently assigned to this cooperative residence.

13

RIVER STREET TO BRIMMER STREET

70 BEACON

This mostly original house was built on new land created by filling the vacant mud flats that were part of the Charles River Basin.

Per an 1828 agreement of the Mount Vernon Proprietors (MVP), Harrison Gray Otis, Jonathan Mason, Benjamin Joy and William Sullivan allocated these flats amongst themselves, as described in the Division of Lands, and filled said lands for the purpose of erecting buildings.

This lot was allocated to Harrison Gray Otis, who proceeded to erect a house. In 1829, the three-story house was one of six (70–75 Beacon) designed by Asher Benjamin,[123] built of granite and very similar in appearance.

This house, which has retained most of its original look, including the purple windowpanes, was sold in 1842 to Dr. John Collins Warren, one of the founders of Massachusetts General Hospital and the first surgeon to use Morton's ether in an operation in 1846.[124] He was the nephew of General Joseph Warren, who was killed in the Battle of Bunker Hill in 1775.

The Warren estate still owned the house in 1860, when the occupant was Thomas Dwight, and that year the house was transferred to Warren's daughter, Mrs. Thomas (Mary Warren) Dwight. The estate retained ownership of the house until 1916, when the property was sold to Josephine C. Forbes, who still owned it as late as 1953.

Today, the house remains a single-family residence.

Looking westward from Brimmer Street, showing six original granite houses starting with 70 Beacon. Some have been heightened, but all relate to their neighbors as originally designed by Asher Benjamin in 1828.

71 BEACON

This mostly original granite house was built between 1829 and 1830 on filled land that was allocated to Harrison Gray Otis. Ownership of the house was transferred in 1835 to Otis's son, William Foster Otis, an attorney, who sold the property. In 1838, it was purchased by Octavius Pickering, author and son of U.S. senator Timothy Pickering. The Pickering family retained the house until 1842, when it was purchased by Henry Greenough, who rented out the house in 1847 to Thomas Motley and Edward Motley Jr., dry goods merchants. Greenough sold the property in 1851 to John Stearns, whose family retained ownership until 1916, when they sold to Frank H. Beebe. The property remained in the Beebe estate until 1950.

Although a fourth story and a roof deck were added at some time, the building still relates to its adjacent three-story neighbors. Today, it is condominiums and is listed as having seven units.

72 BEACON

This residence is one of six granite houses built between 1829 and 1830, designed by Asher Benjamin and allocated in 1828 to Benjamin Joy. In 1833, John F. Loring, administrator of Joy's estate, sold the house and land to Thomas Cordis, who sold the house in 1854 to Hannah Russell. It was then transferred to Mary A. Russell. After Mary's death, the property was devised to her daughters, Alice Fitzgerald and Edith Playfair of London, England.

In 1918, the property was sold by Edith Playfair and Alice Fitzgerald to Frank H. Beebe, who also owned 71 Beacon, with which this property was connected for a time. The Beebe estate retained ownership of the house until it was sold in 1946 to Edward N. Fenno, who still owned in 1953.

Today, the property is listed as a three-family residence.

73 BEACON

This Asher Benjamin–designed granite house was one of six built between 1829 and 1830. The house was constructed on land allocated in 1828 to William Sullivan, a son-in-law of Mrs. Hepzibah Swan, whom he represented, in the MVP's Division of Lands. Sullivan sold the house in 1833 to Henry J. Sargent, attorney, along with lots seventy-six and eighty-three.

The house remained in the Sargent family until 1902, when Francis W. Sargent sold it to Ellen C. and Charles E. Loud, who owned it until 1943, when they sold to Adelaide C. Sohier. Sohier resided there until 1950, when the house was sold to Dorothy P.D. Putnam. Putnam lived there until at least 1953.

Today, the building is condominiums with two units.

74 BEACON

This is one of six granite houses designed by Asher Benjamin and built between 1829 and 1830 by members of the MVP. This house was erected on land allocated to Jonathan Mason. Under the terms of Mason's 1831 will, the house was devised to his daughter, Miriam C. (Sears), wife of David Sears II.

In 1835, the house belonged to David and Miriam Sears and was being rented to Eppes Sargent. Sears continued to rent the house to various people, including John Pickering, Alfred Greenough and Wolsley Borland,

and in 1857 Sears sold the dwelling to Thomas P. Rich, of Rich, Townsend & Cowing, auctioneers and commission merchants.

In 1875, Rich sold the house to Mary E. Abbott, and in 1890 M.W. Abbott sold to Nina (Mrs. William) Appleton, whose family retained ownership as late as 1938, when the trustees, under the will of William Appleton, sold to Grace Post Eddy, who owned it until 1946.

Today, the building has a fourth story, added sometime subsequent to 1875, and is residential. It comprises four to six family units.

75 BEACON

This is the westernmost of the six granite houses designed by Asher Benjamin and built by members of the MVP. The land was allocated to Jonathan Mason in 1828 under the Division of Lands, and as early as 1835 the property was transferred to Mason's son, William P. Mason, who rented out the house to various people, including John Pickering, Benjamin Curtis, Edward A. Crowninshield and Thomas E. Chickering of Chickering & Sons, pianoforte manufacturers.

In 1875, William Mason was living in the house, and in 1884 he sold the dwelling to Henrietta (Wigglesworth) Holmes, wife of Edward Jackson

Numbers 78, 77, 76 and 75 Beacon, circa 1870. Number 76 Beacon was replaced in 1906 with a granite house to continue the flow of the original Benjamin design. *Courtesy of Boston Athenaeum.*

Holmes, younger brother of United States Supreme Court justice Oliver Wendell Holmes.

Following the death of Edward, Henrietta married Walter Scott Fitz,[125] a successful China trade merchant who in 1873 became a partner in Russell & Co.'s Hong Kong office. Henrietta was his second wife (his first had been her sister, Anna C. Wigglesworth). Fitz wrote an account of "the most eventful journey in the history of railroading" when taking an 1872 transcontinental train trip that was scheduled to take less than a week and instead turned into a thirty-six-day, storm-filled trip.[126]

In 1936, Henrietta's estate sold to Edward T.P. Graham, architect, who had designed the Forsyth Dental Infirmary and St. Paul Catholic Church in Cambridge, Massachusetts. Graham owned the property as late as 1953, when it was listed as having fifteen rooms and four baths.

Today, the building is being used for apartments.

76 BEACON

This granite house replaced the original brick house built on filled land allocated to William Sullivan. In 1833, Sullivan sold the lot to Henry J. Sargent, and in 1845 Sargent sold the site to Dr. John C. Warren, who proceeded, in 1847, to build a house that was occupied by his newly married daughter Emily and her husband, William (Warren) Appleton.

The family owned the property until 1906, when it was sold to Amy G. Iasigi, widow of Oscar Iasigi, former consul general to the Ottoman Empire. He was lost at sea with the sinking of the *City of Columbus* in 1884 off the coast of Martha's Vineyard. Mrs. Iasigi removed the existing house and in 1906 erected a new one, designed by architect A.W. Longfellow. This new structure was a five-story residence, with the front constructed of granite to complement 70–75 Beacon.

In 1928, Iasigi sold the house to Alice L.T. (Mrs. Robert H.) Stevenson, who owned it as late as 1953, when the house was listed as having seventeen rooms. Today, it is listed as a two-family residence.

77 BEACON

This remarkably unchanged brick house was built on filled land allocated by the MVP to Benjamin Joy. In 1835, the lot belonged to the estate of Benjamin Joy, and in 1854 a house built by James Standish, mason, was purchased by Henry Sigourney, merchant.

Sigourney, his wife Amelie Louise (Rives) and three of their children perished at sea in 1873, when the ocean liner *Ville de Havre* sank off the coast of Newfoundland following a collision with another ship. Two additional children, including Henry Jr., survived, as they hadn't traveled with their parents on that terrible voyage. Amelie Louise was the sister of William Cabell Rives Jr., who married Grace Winthrop Sears and lived at 41 Beacon.

The Sigourney family retained ownership of the house until 1947. Today, the building is listed as a residential and commercial property.

78 BEACON

The house erected here was built on filled land allocated to Jonathan Mason. In 1845, the lot of land was still vacant, and in 1846, Mason sold the property, with a dwelling house, to Edward A. Crowninshield, son of Secretary of the Navy Benjamin W. Crowninshield. Edward was a lover of rare books, and his library was described by George S. Hillard as having "some of the most beautiful and desirable books we have seen, books such as it was difficult to look at without breaking the tenth Commandment."[127]

In 1856, Edward Crowninshield sold to Gardiner G. Hammond, who remained the owner of the property until 1872, when he sold to Anna H.

Numbers 81, 80, 79, 78 and 77 Beacon, circa 1870. Number 80 Beacon was altered in 1936, when a fifth floor was added, while 81 Beacon, on the far left, was razed and replaced with the new ten-floor building seen today. *Courtesy of Boston Athenaeum.*

Mason. In 1885, Mason sold to George G. Hall, hotelier, who owned the famed Adams House Hotel. In 1938, the house belonged to Laura G. Hall.

In 1940, Laura Hall sold the property to Arthur C. and Eleanor J. Sullivan, who owned it until at least 1953, when the residence was listed in tax records as having fifteen rooms. Although the façade has been changed and an additional story has been added to the house, it still relates to its abutters.

Today, the building remains a single-family residence.

79 BEACON

This building was built on filled land that was allocated to Jonathan Mason. In 1840, the empty lot belonged to Jonathan Mason's daughter, Mary B. (Mason) Parkman, wife of Samuel Parkman, the son of Dr. George Parkman. In 1848, Parkman, acting for the Jonathan Mason estate, sold the property, with an unfinished house on it, to William R. Rodman. In that same year, Rodman sold the finished house to Samuel Whitwell and his brother, Henry, of S.H. Whitwell Co., importers. They retained ownership until 1864.

In 1864, the Whitwells sold the house to George B. Upton, merchant. Upton was a sponsor of the Boston & European Steamship Co., along with Donald MacKay, Andrew Hall and James M. Beebe, and was named as one of the house flags carried by Donald MacKay's famous clipper ships. In 1882, Upton sold the property to William D. Sohier, attorney.

In 1927, Sohier sold the property, and in 1928 the new owner was Augustus L. Putnam.

Putnam owned the property until 1946, when the building was sold to Madelaine C. Whiting, trustee for Charles G. Whiting, at which time the house was listed in tax records as having sixteen rooms and five baths.

Today, the building houses five condominium units.

80 BEACON

This building replaced the house originally built here, constructed on filled land allocated to Harrison Gray Otis. Otis sold the lot in 1846 to Charles Mifflin, physician, who proceeded to erect a house, which he owned until 1873, when he sold to Patrick Grant.

In 1896, Grant sold to S. Eliot Guild, who in turn sold the property, in 1901, to Fannie M. Faulkner. Faulkner was still residing in the house in 1928, per *Clarke's Blue Book*. In 1936, the house was sold to James S. Smith, and in the same year a variance was issued by the Boston Building Department allowing the owner to remodel it, adding a fifth floor and creating an apartment building.

Today, the building houses ten residential condominiums.

81 BEACON

This ten-floor apartment building, erected in 1925, replaced the original house built on filled land allocated to Harrison Gray Otis.

In 1847, Otis sold the empty lot to the Jonathan Mason estate, and the property is listed in the city tax records as a "house building." In 1851, the Mason estate sold the house and land to William Appleton.

Appleton sold the property in 1857 to Dr. Edward Wigglesworth, a physician for diseases of the skin at the Boston City Hospital. In 1899, his widow, Sarah Wigglesworth, transferred the house to Mary G. Pickering and Jane N. (Wigglesworth) Grew, who married J. Pierpont Morgan Jr., son of the famous banker.

In 1909, Pickering and Grew sold the house to Louis B. Thacher (Henry C. Thacher had purchased 82 Beacon in 1891).

In 1925, Louis B. Thacher sold the house to James H. Ripley of a real estate trust that was acquiring both 81 and 82 Beacon and planning to replace them with

Numbers 81, 80 and 79 Beacon. Number 81 Beacon replaced the earlier structures of 82 and 81 Beacon in 1925.

a ten-floor apartment building. Both the original houses were razed and replaced with an apartment building designed by J.D. Leland.

Today, the owner is 81 Beacon Street Corporation, and the property remains an apartment building.

82 BEACON

The original house erected here was built on filled land allocated to Benjamin Joy and was replaced, in 1925, by a ten-story residential building now 81 Beacon. In 1854, Joy's estate sold the empty lot at auction to Tisdale Drake, of Tisdale Drake & Son, who was in the wood and coal business. In 1855, a house had been erected on the property, and in 1876 the widow of Tisdale Drake sold the property to Seth E. Pecker.

Pecker, of Seth E. Pecker & Co., liquor and wine dealer, lived in the house, and in 1891 the estate sold it to Henry C. Thacher.

Numbers 84, 83 and 82 Beacon, circa 1870. Brimmer Street is on the left. Numbers 84 and 83 Beacon were replaced by the Bayard Thayer House in 1911. *Copyright © John F. Kennedy Library Foundation.*

In 1925, Thomas B. and Louis B. Thacher sold the original house to James H. Ripley, who also owned 81 Beacon. Shortly thereafter, the house was removed, along with 81 Beacon, and replaced by the existing ten-story apartment building designed by architect J.D. Leland.

83 BEACON

The original house here was built on filled land created from the flats and allocated to William Sullivan, who was a son-in-law of MVP proprietor Hepzibah Swan.

In 1833, the empty lot was sold to John T. Sargent, and in 1849 the property was sold to Benjamin Mussey, bookseller and real estate developer. Mussey then entered into an agreement with James Standish, mason and house builder, to erect a house on the site. In 1850, the completed house was sold to Edward Codman, grocer and wine merchant.

In 1881, the house was sold by the heirs of Edward Codman to J. Arthur Beebe, who resided there until 1892, when he sold the property to Augustus P. Gardner. Gardner, a United States congressman from 1902 to 1917, had been raised by his aunt Isabella Stewart Gardner of Fenway Court. His estate sold in 1895 to Fifty Associates, a real estate investment firm, and in 1910 the house was sold by Fifty Associates to Boston native Bayard Thayer.

In 1911, Thayer replaced the original house (along with 84 Beacon) with the Manhattan-style mansion designed by Ogden Codman that still stands today.

In 1943, the Ruth S. Thayer estate sold the mansion to John R. Watson, trustee for Colonial Properties, and in 1945 the building housed six apartments with forty-four rooms.

Although this number is no longer affixed to any building on Beacon Street, it is used by the tax department as the "parcel address" for 84 Beacon.

THE HAMPSHIRE HOUSE

84 Beacon

This grand mansion, today's Hampshire House, was constructed on two city lots and replaced the house originally built on filled land allocated to Harrison Gray Otis.

By 1845, Otis built a house and rented it to Judge Samuel Hubbard. In 1855, the house was occupied by Otis's grandson, Harrison Ritchie, lawyer. In 1870, Ritchie sold the property for the estate to William Gardner Prescott, son of historian William H. Prescott.

In 1895, Prescott sold the property to Fifty Associates, and in 1910 that company sold the building to Bayard Thayer.

Thayer then razed the existing house, along with 83 Beacon, and replaced it with a new Georgian revival town house designed by Ogden Codman. Covering two lots, this new house was one of the largest single-family residences constructed in the Beacon Hill area and seemed more appropriate for New York City than for conservative Boston.

Thayer was renowned for his yachting sportsmanship, having entered the America's Cup races in the 1890s. He was also a noted arboriculturist,

Numbers 84 and 81 Beacon. The Bayard Thayer mansion at 84 Beacon today is the popular Hampshire House, which retains much of the original elegance of the Thayer home.

having created on his 217-acre estate in Lancaster, Massachusetts, a pinetum, which contained representatives of every coniferous plant that can grow in Massachusetts.[128] He was also an avid hunter and had at one time a game preserve of several thousand acres into which he introduced, for the first time in these parts, the English game pheasant.[129] Codman was a renowned architect and interior decorator who had collaborated with Edith Wharton on a definitive book titled *Decoration of Houses*, published in 1897.

Through Wharton, Codman met Cornelius Vanderbilt II and was hired to decorate rooms in Vanderbilt's Newport mansion, the Breakers.

In 1938, the house belonged to Bayard Thayer's heirs, and in 1943 the executors of the Ruth S. Thayer estate sold to John R. Watson, trustee of Colonial Properties, Inc.

> *The Hampshire House acquired its name during World War II when…it was leased as a small private luxury hotel to the owners of the Lincolnshire Hotel on Charles Street. They dubbed the mansion the Hampshire House (Lincolnshire and Hampshire being both English counties).[130]*

Today, the building, which retains much of its original elegance, uses the address eighty-four and is home to the popular Hampshire House Restaurant. The Bull & Finch Pub, made famous by the television series *Cheers*, is located in the basement level.

Brimmer Street to Beaver Street

85 Beacon

The house originally standing here was erected on filled land and was allocated by the Mount Vernon Proprietors (MVP) to Jonathan Mason. In 1834, under the partition of the Jonathan Mason estate by the court of common pleas, the empty lot was partitioned off to David Sears.

In 1845, Sears had a house built on the site and rented it out to an attorney, Sidney Morse. In 1855, the tenant in the house was Nathaniel Curtis of the firm of Curtis, Bouvé & Co., commission merchants.

In 1872, the owner was Frederick S.G. D'Hautville, son of Ellen Sears D'Hautville (daughter of David Sears II), who had married a Swiss citizen and briefly moved to Switzerland.

In 1910, the property belonged to H.F. Sears, and the original three-story dwelling was razed, along with 86 Beacon, to make way for a new larger house. This double lot mansion was designed by architect Haven Wheelwright.

86 Beacon

This large mansion, built in 1910, was the home of Dr. Henry F. Sears, son of David Sears II. The house, which covers two lots—as does its neighbor 84 Beacon, the Bayard Thayer House—was designed by the firm of Haven and Wheelwright, which also designed the Boston Opera House (now

Above: Numbers 87, 86 and 85 Beacon, circa 1870. In 1910, 86 and 85 Beacon were razed to make way for the Sears House. *Copyright © John F. Kennedy Library Foundation.*

Left: Built in 1910 and originally the home of Frederick R. Sears, this mansion rivaled its neighbor, 84 Beacon, the Bayard Thayer House.

demolished) and the Larz Anderson Bridge that crosses the Charles River from Boston into Cambridge.

This house replaced the one first erected here, built on filled land created by the MVP and allocated to Benjamin Joy, whose family owned the empty lot. In 1854, this property, as part of the estate of Benjamin Joy, was sold at public auction to David Sears II.

In 1856, there was a four-story house here that remained on the site until 1910. At that time, it was owned by Henry F. and Jean Irvine Sears, who removed it, along with 85 Beacon, in order to make way for the present mansion, which retains the address 86 Beacon.

In 1942, Henry Sears sold the house to the Charlotte Cushman Club of Boston, and the mansion was listed as having forty rooms and seven baths. Charlotte Cushman was a famous nineteenth-century actress and philanthropist. At the height of her career in the 1830s, she was called America's greatest tragic actress, long remembered for her role as Lady Macbeth.

The club was a residence for actresses, their motto being "a home away from home for women of the theatre." Honoring Cushman's contributions, the City of Boston built a school named for her on the site of her birthplace.

Number 86 Beacon was later the site of the women's career educational school, the Katherine Gibbs School, until the building was converted into condominiums.

Today, the building houses four condominium units, with the ground floor belonging to the Greek Consulate of Boston.

87 Beacon

This house was erected on land created by filling in the flats and was the westernmost portion of the MVP purchase from Copley in 1796. In the MVP 1828 Division of Lands, this lot was allocated to Harrison Gray Otis and was sold in 1829 to John Sanderson. It was triangular in shape, with the western side marked by a sea wall that the MVP had built to delineate its property (the flats) that they were filling in and to prevent the tides from flooding the land.

In 1830, Sanderson sold a half interest in the lot, which was composed of "land, wharfrights, flats and waterrights," to Jesse Shaw, housewright, and tax records for that year show that there was a bathhouse on the land. In 1835, Shaw and Sanderson sold their interests in this property to the Boston & Roxbury Mill Corporation. A portion of the property was sold in 1846 to

Andrew T. Hall, president of the Tremont Bank, who built a house in 1848 and retained ownership until 1884.

In 1884, Hall sold the property to Alice M. Burnham, who erected a new house on the site, replacing the original three-story bow-front residence. This new dwelling is the house we see today.

The house stayed in the Burnham family until 1923, and in 1928 it belonged to Helen O. Storrow. Mrs. James Storrow, who was known for her philanthropy, conveyed the property, in 1934, to the Massachusetts Girl Scouts Inc., which owned it as late as 1953.

Today, the building houses eight condominium units.

88 BEACON

This original house was part of a quadruple row house, 88, 89, 90 and 91 Beacon, built on land filled by the Boston & Roxbury Mill Corporation in the 1840s. In 1846, the corporation sold the land to Sidney Morse, who in turn sold the empty lot, incorporating the adjacent parcel, 89 Beacon, in 1851 to John Foster, a builder. This purchase gave Foster, along with his earlier purchase of the land that would become 90 and 91 Beacon from W. Stone, a total frontage of ninety-six feet on Beacon that would become 88, 89, 90 and 91 Beacon.

Numbers 91, 90, 89 and 88 Beacon. These quadruple row houses remain essentially the same today, except for the relocation of the entrance stairs of 91 and 90 to the ground level. *Copyright © John F. Kennedy Library Foundation.*

Foster and his associate, James Standish, erected this house, along with 89 Beacon, in 1852, and in 1854 it was owned by Samuel R. Payson, a commission merchant of dry goods.

The Payson family continued to occupy the house into the twentieth century, and in 1914 Hannah R. Payson sold the house to Robert Jordan, who in turn sold it to Oliver Ames in 1922. Ames conveyed the house the next year, 1923, to his daughter, Mrs. William Amory Parker. Ames was active in his family's business, Oliver Ames & Sons, the firm that had contributed to the transcontinental railroad with the famous "Ames shovel." He also participated in the growth of the General Electric Company.[131]

In 1937, William Parker sold to Waldron P. Belknap, who owned the property as late as 1953, when the building was described as having five apartments.

This house still retains the original exterior entry stairway leading to the first floor and today is condominiums, with six units.

89 BEACON

This original dwelling house was erected on filled land created by the Boston & Roxbury Mill Corporation and sold in 1846 to Sidney R. Morse, who in turn sold it, along with an adjacent parcel, in 1851 to John Foster.

Foster and James Standish erected this house and sold it in 1852 to Emily Taylor Parker. In 1864, it was sold to David Sears.

Under the will of David Sears, the house remained in the Frederick R. Sears family until 1874, when it was sold to Jane N. Grew. In the 1890s, Mr. and Mrs. Henry Grew were living in the house. In 1922, the property was purchased by Katherine H. Putnam, who still owned it as late as 1953.

Today, the building is an apartment house.

90 BEACON

This mostly original house was one of the four identical ones built on land filled by the Boston & Roxbury Mill Corporation in the 1840s and sold by that company in 1847. In 1852, the owners were Charles J. Fox, mason, of Turner and Fox, house builders. In 1854, James Read, a dry goods commission merchant, purchased the house.

Around the turn of the century, the entry stairway leading from the ground to the first floor was eliminated and the ground floor became the entry level. This change provided more usable space in the building and was possible because of the modern plumbing designs allowing living space on the ground level.

James Read willed the property to his daughters, Lucy Richmond Read and Sara Elizabeth Read, and subsequently it was conveyed, in 1911, to Shepherd Brooks, an architect and husband of Read's granddaughter, Clara Gardner. In Medford, Brooks built Acorn Hill, a manor, on his family's seventeenth-century estate, and today it is part of the Medford-Brooks Estate Land Trust that is open to the public. In 1914, Brooks transferred ownership to his daughter, Rachel B. Jackson, who owned it until 1941.

In 1941, the property was purchased by the Henry George Institute of New England, which retained it (having changed its name to the Free Market Institute in 1947) until 1952.

The Henry George Institute taught programs espousing tax and land reform and was founded by Henry George, a famous and controversial economist.

In 1979, the building was converted into condominiums from an apartment house. Today, the building houses seven condominiums.

91 BEACON

This house, whose façade is mostly original, was built on filled land created by the Boston & Roxbury Mill Corporation. In 1851, the owners were Turner and Fox, builders, who proceeded to erect this house and 90 Beacon. In 1852, the completed house was sold by Fox to Richard T. Parker.

In 1863, the property was sold by Parker to Josiah B. Bardwell, and in 1871 ownership was in the name Ellen Brooks. The house remained in the Brooks family. In 1914, Shepherd Brooks transferred the property to his daughter, Helen B. Emmons, who retained ownership until 1941. In 1915, the main entrance was dropped to ground level and the staircase eliminated.

In 1942, the property was divided into two lots: "A," the rear section, and "B," the section fronting on Beacon Street and composing most of the original house. Today, the building is classified as a three-family residence.

15

BEAVER STREET TO EMBANKMENT ROAD (OTTER STREET)

92 BEACON

This twenty-unit apartment building built in the 1940s replaced the house first built here, erected on land filled by the Boston & Roxbury Mill Corporation.

The original house was sold in 1847 to William Ropes, of W. Ropes & Co., merchants, located on Lewis Wharf, and was one of eight similar residences designed by well-known architect and builder George M. Dexter.[132]

At the same time, in 1847 the Boston & Roxbury Mill Corporation signed an indenture concerning the lots where it agreed to build River, Beacon and Otter Streets (now Embankment Road), and per an agreement with G. Dexter, the houses built on these lots would have the same façade and the same setback from the street.

In 1869, the house was sold by Ropes to Shepherd Brooks, who later owned both 90 and 91 Beacon. In 1940, Clara Brooks's executors sold the dwelling to Beacon-Beaver, Inc. This company then proceeded to raze the existing house and in its place erected the six-floor apartment building that exists today.

In 1943, Beacon-Beaver, Inc. sold the property to Lilly L. Benson, who owned it as late as 1953.

Today, the building houses twenty condominium units.

Left: Number 92 Beacon. This six-floor condominium was built in 1940 as apartments and replaced the 1847 dwelling that was one of eight similar row houses designed by George M. Dexter.

Below: This photograph, taken from the Public Garden circa 1880, shows 99, 98, 97, 96, 95, 94, 93 and 92 Beacon, the eight Dexter row houses on the far left, and 91–86 Beacon on the right. *Courtesy of the Bostonian Society/Old State House Museum.*

93 BEACON

This house, whose façade is mostly original, was one of the eight houses (92–99 Beacon) erected in a row and designed and built by George M. Dexter. It was sold by the Boston & Roxbury Mill Corporation in 1847 to Benjamin R. Curtis, a United States Court judge and lawyer who retained ownership until 1852, when he sold it to William Appleton.

Appleton rented out the house in 1855, and the occupant was the great-grandson of President Thomas Jefferson, Thomas Jefferson Coolidge, minister to France under Benjamin Harrison. In 1860, William transferred the property to his son, Charles H. Appleton, who conveyed the house in 1862 to his sister, Hetty S. Coolidge (Mrs. Thomas Jefferson Coolidge). It remained in the Coolidge family until 1897, when it was sold to Clara Gardner Brooks, who also owned 92 Beacon.

The house remained in the Brooks family until 1927, when Gorham Brooks sold to George Cabot Lee, a banker, who retained the property until 1940, when he sold to Jenny K. Gegan. Gegan owned it as late as 1953, and the property was listed as being apartments and rooms.

Today, the building houses apartments.

94 BEACON

This mostly original house was built on land filled by the Boston & Roxbury Mill Corporation in the 1840s and sold as vacant land in 1847 to Arthur L. Payson. The house was designed by George M. Dexter and was one of eight similar row houses (92–99 Beacon).

The house remained in the Payson family until 1860, when John L. Payson, merchant, sold the property. In 1867, Annie B. Fay owned it, and in 1880 the dwelling belonged to Anna B.F. Matthews.

In 1945, the building was owned by Vincent M. Cantella, a real estate investor, who sold it in 1949 to Clifford Speed. Speed owned it as late as 1953.

Today, the property is a five-unit condominium building.

95 BEACON

This house was one of eight in a row (92–99 Beacon) designed by George M. Dexter. This site was filled land created by the Boston & Roxbury Mill

Corporation and was sold in 1847 to Sidney Bartlett, attorney, who retained ownership until 1891.

In 1891, the Bartlett family sold the house to Henry Lee, who in turn sold it in 1909 to Jane Norton Grew, wife of John Pierpont Morgan Jr., son of J.P. Morgan of banking fame.

In 1911, the property was transferred to Jane Norton Grew's sister, Henrietta van Rensselaer Crosby, who still owned it in 1953.

The original dwelling was altered early in the twentieth century while retaining its original height and flat façade. Today, the building houses twelve condominium units.

96 BEACON

This was one of the eight row houses (92–99 Beacon) designed by George M. Dexter and erected on filled land. It was sold by the Boston & Roxbury Mill Corporation in 1847 to Dexter. In 1849, Dexter was assessed for a "house unfinished," and in 1850 he sold the house to William Shimmin, treasurer of the Dover (New Hampshire) manufacturing company that was one of the first textile companies to print calico and other cottons in the United States.

In 1873, the Charles F. Shimmin estate sold the property to Henry Lee, whose heirs remained owners until at least 1908. Lee also later owned 95 Beacon; however, it was in this house that he resided.

In 1913, the house was owned by Henry D. and Johanna H. Burnham. They remained in possession until 1947, when the house was listed as closed. In 1948, the new owner was the Engineers Club, Massachusetts Co., which owned it until at least 1953.

This building, while substantially remodeled, retains the height of the original. Today, it belongs to Emerson College and is the westernmost edifice still existing of the original row of eight houses.

97 BEACON

The house that originally existed with this number was one of eight houses in a row (92–99 Beacon) designed by George M. Dexter and erected on land filled by the Boston & Roxbury Mill Corporation. It was sold in 1849 to George T. Curtis. In 1850, Curtis's house was completed, and in 1854 he sold the property to trustees for Robert G. Shaw.

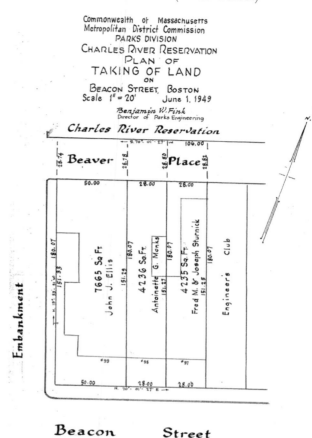

Commonwealth of Massachusetts
Metropolitan District Commission
PARKS DIVISION
CHARLES RIVER RESERVATION
PLAN OF
TAKING OF LAND
ON
BEACON STREET, BOSTON
Scale 1" = 20'   June 1, 1949

Benjamin W. Fink
Director of Parks Engineering

The 1949 Plan of Taking by the Commonwealth of Massachusetts of numbers 99, 98 and 87 Beacon. These buildings were removed in 1950, when Embankment Road was widened and the entrance to Storrow Drive was created.

In 1859, the owner was Henry V. Ward, treasurer of the Lawrence, Tremont and Suffolk Manufacturing Co. and the Chilean consul in Boston. He was the owner until 1869, when he sold the property to Edward Brooks.

In 1892, Louise Brooks conveyed the property to George A. Gardner, and in 1901 George A. Gardner sold to Marian P. Motley.

In 1938, the house still belonged to Marian P. Motley, who retained ownership until 1947, when the house was listed as closed and was sold.

In September 1949, the property was taken by the Commonwealth of Massachusetts by eminent domain for highway purposes.

The house was removed in 1950 when Embankment Road, formerly Otter Street, was widened and the entrance to Storrow Drive was created. Storrow Drive was named in honor of Boston philanthropist James Jackson Storrow, whose efforts helped in creating the Charles River embankment.

98 BEACON

The house that originally had this address was one of eight in a row (92–99 Beacon) designed by George M. Dexter and built on land filled by the Boston & Roxbury Mill Corporation. The house was sold in 1851 to Amos Lawrence of Amos A. Lawrence & Co., domestic goods. In 1852, it was occupied by Amos's brother, William R. Lawrence, physician, who sold it in 1861 to William W. Tucker of Upham, Tucker & Co., commission merchants.

Tucker remained as owner until 1883, when he sold to T. Quincy Brown. In 1889, Brown sold the house to Dudley L. Pickman, a trustee of the Museum of Fine Arts and one of its most generous benefactors.

The house remained in the Pickman family until 1941, when it was sold. In August of the same year, the owner was Antoinette Monks. It remained in her possession until it was taken in 1949 by the Commonwealth of Massachusetts for highway purposes. The house was removed in 1950, when the Storrow Drive entrance was created.

99 BEACON

The house that was originally at this address was one of eight (92–99 Beacon) designed by George M. Dexter and built by the Boston & Roxbury Mill Corporation. It was sold in 1852 to William W. Goddard of Goddard and Thompson, merchants. In 1871, Goddard sold the house to John W. Draper and Oliver Ditson, owner of a well-known music store. In 1873, John W. Draper sold to Harriet J.G. Denny, and in 1879 the house was sold by Denny to Emily S. Spaulding.

John T. Spaulding and his wife, Emily, retained ownership until 1949, when the Metropolitan District Commission for the Commonwealth of Massachusetts took the property. "Spaulding left an extraordinary collection [of art] to the [Museum of Fine Arts], including paintings by Manet, Matisse, Van Gogh, Renoir, Cezanne, and Degas—all of which had adorned his…home.[133]

In 1950, the house was removed when Embankment Road was widened and the entrance to Storrow Drive was created.

Appendix A

Numbering

The current numbering system of the addresses on Beacon Street was adopted in 1866 as a result of the previous confusion of accurate house numbering that started when Boston first became a city in 1822. Prior to 1822, houses were not numbered in any significant order but were described by their current or previous owners or, in some cases, by their prominence or historic stature.

The first actual record of dwellings was officially recorded by the selectmen of Boston, as shown in the *Book of Possessions*. The book was a document covering four years, from 1645 to 1648, and described the properties in the town of Boston and the owners. For example, one entry read:

> *The possession of Mr. John Cotton within the Limits of Boston*
> *One house and garden, about halfe an Acre, with an Acre adjoyneinge, bounded with Sudbury streete on the east; Edward Bendall on the north; the Centry hill on the west; and Mr. Bellingham and Daniel Maude on the south.*[134]

It was not until 1789, following the American Revolution, that a true list of inhabitants and the location of their residences was published as *The Boston Directory*. This directory would be continuously published throughout the eighteenth and nineteenth centuries and well into the twentieth.

The third directory, published in 1798, was corroborated by the first United States description of all inhabitants and their residences in the nation. This listing was compiled due to the 1798 Federal Act, the result of which was a record of all dwellings in the country (including, of course, Boston), their values and their owners, providing us with the first list of houses in all the states that were part of the Union.

As stated, the houses on Beacon Street were not numbered until 1822, and at that time the numbers started at the west end at Charles Street and went up as the addresses progressed east toward Tremont Street. For example, today's 64 Beacon, the King's Chapel House, was One Beacon originally.

This system must have proved unworkable, as new buildings were going up in between existing numbers, causing changes in existing number succession. Thus, in 1824, Boston City Council records show that a committee was set up to "see about changing names and numbering of streets."[135]

In 1830, the numbering was reversed, with One Beacon starting at Tremont Street and increasing as the houses went westward toward Charles Street. It was at about this time that all the addresses on Beacon Street were given numbers. But problems continued, as noted in the *Boston Directory of 1850–1851*, published by George Adams. There was an appeal to the City of Boston to revise its numbering policy to include potential future buildings. In its then current form, when a new building was erected on an open space, all the existing numbers had to be changed to accommodate the numerical alignment. This old system accounts for many of the buildings numbered "one-half," such as the Boston Athenaeum at 10½ Beacon.

This arrangement of numbering continued until 1866, when the numbers on the south side of Beacon Street between Tremont and Park Streets were officially changed for a final time as a result of a city order.

One of the few exceptions happened with the construction of the new headquarters for the Unitarian Association, which replaced 31 Beacon. The association had sold its old building, Channing Hall (then 25 Beacon), at the corner of Beacon and Bowdoin Streets and, when moving, requested of the city the right to use the same number again. The city granted this request.

The following numbers are no longer used as addresses by the City of Boston:

2	26	37½	97
3	27	38	98
4	28	47	99
5	29	68	
7	30	82	
13	30½	83	
23	31	85	

STREETS

F rom the earliest times, the first settlers of Boston recognized the importance of what was to become Beacon Street. Known first as the Lane to Centry Hill and later as the Lane to the Almshouse, Beacon Street was the road to the hill upon which was located the emergency beacon to warn the town's inhabitants of a real or impending emergency. Since most of the settlers were congregating in the dock and harbor area, the street to the warning beacon had to be an open lane: "Also it is ordered that the streete from Mr. Atherton Haulghes to the Centry hill to be layd out, so kept open forever."[136] Mr. Hough (Haulghes) resided at the south corner of today's School and Washington Streets; consequently, the foregoing order established the whole of School Street as well as part of Beacon Street.[137]

In the town of Boston, the actual laying out of streets was a result of an effort by the settlement to ensure that every person should have access to his allotment of land. This started the creation of streets, with many of them having general names such as highway, lane or path and others taking the name of some person's house or some notable location.

It wasn't until 1708 that current names were given to these streets. At a meeting of the selectmen on May 3, 1708,

> *it was ordered that the streets,* lanes, alleys of this town as they are now bounded and named be accordingly recorded in the Town Booke which are as followeth:[138]

BEACON STREET—the way leading from Mrs. Whetcomb's corner to the house of Capt. Fairwether westerly through the upper side of the Common and so down to the sea.

CENTRY STREET—The way leading from Beacon Street between Capt. Alford's land and Madam Shrimpton's pasture up to Centry Hill. Later known as Park Street.

COMMON STREET—The way leading from Melynes' [Melyen's] corner near Coll. Townsend's corner.

TRAMOUNT STREET—The way leading from the mansion house of the late Simon Lynde, Esq. by Capt. Southack's extending as far as Col. Townsend's corner.

The streets around which our story revolves did not always keep the same names, however. Centry Street became Park Street, Common Street became Tremont Street and Tramount Street became part of Common Street.

As our friend Gleaner wrote in a chapter titled "Names of Streets":

Few matters of mere taste and fashion result in more serious inconveniences than the frequent and capricious changes made in the names of streets. Our original street nomenclature was certainly not very select, yet how interesting would it be to the local antiquarian to feel sure at once of the identity of some old locality from its existing name! How many spots in London are still visited by pilgrims who delight to recall the wits and sages who formerly frequented them!

Our Pudding lane, *so called, probably, from some primitive eating-house, had not ceased to be an appropriate designation even in the days of the Exchange Coffee-house—though it had long been superseded by* Devonshire street. Frog lane, *so named from the ancient croakers on the Common, though now called* Boylston street, *will, I understand, in view of the very latest improvements, be officially changed to* "Squirrel avenue."

An old gentleman once told me that he had always lived in the same house, but on six different streets. *It fronted easterly on Orange street, afterwards Washington street, and bounded northerly on Nassau street, afterwards Common street, then Tremont street, and finally Common street again, after Tremont street was extended through to meet Tremont road. An individual who devotes himself to the examination of land titles may, indeed, well sigh at these changes.*[139]

In order to allow the reader to follow old maps and ancient descriptions more easily, following are some of the existing and changed names that might be encountered:

ARLINGTON STREET, 1858: From opposite 95 Beacon Street to 321 Boylston Street. It is shown as eighty feet wide on a plan dated 1854.

BEACON STREET, 1708: Known from the earliest times as the lane to Centry Hill and later as the Lane to the Almshouse:

> *Name first given to Beacon Street in 1708—from Tremont Street over Beacon Hill, passing the Common, and over the former Mill-dam of the Boston and Roxbury Mill Corporation; the part of the present Beacon Street, from Tremont Street to a point near the corner of Beacon Street and Somerset Street, formed part of School Street, 1708; released by the B&R Mill Corp. to the Commonwealth of Massachusetts by indenture of June 9, 1854, "to be forever kept open as a public highway."*[140]

BEAVER STREET, 1857: From Beacon Street nearly opposite Arlington Street north to unnamed street (Beaver Place). It was accepted, conditionally, from Beacon Street north to the water (Charles River) on July 1, 1857.

BELKNAP STREET: See Joy Street.

BOWDOIN STREET: First named in 1805 after Governor John Bowdoin, whose mansion house was located on the easterly side of the street; from Beacon Street to Cambridge Street. The part from Cambridge Street to near present-day Derne Street was laid out as a forty-foot street in 1727, later known as Middlecott Street. Bowdoin's son continued the street through to Beacon Street circa 1805 and renamed it Bowdoin Street.

BRIMMER STREET, 1866: From Pinckney Street to Beacon Street. The part between Chestnut Street and Beacon Street was called D Street in 1828. This part was named Messenger Street on January 5, 1856. The name of Messenger Street was changed to Brimmer Street on April 20, 1869.

CHARLES STREET: Recognized by the town in 1805, from Boylston Street (formerly Frog Lane) opposite Park Square to Leverett Street. Permission to form and complete one hundred feet of new street from Pleasant Street to Beacon Street parallel with the ropewalks (which ran between what is now the Common and the Public Garden) was granted on July 6, 1803. The street was laid out from Beacon Street to Cambridge Street in 1805.

COMMON STREET: See Tremont Street.

D STREET, 1828: From Mill Dam (now Beacon Street) north to the water. Established in 1828 from Western Avenue (now Beacon Street) to Chestnut Street and accepted on August 7, 1855. It had the same name as Messenger Street on January 15, 1856, but changed to Brimmer Street in 1869.

FREEMAN PLACE, 1846: From Beacon Street north between Somerset and Bowdoin Streets to the west of 15 Beacon. This street originally served as a lane to the Unitarian Church known as the Church of the Disciples. This chapel was built under the auspices of the Reverend James Freeman Clarke.

GEORGE STREET, 1732: From Beacon street north, to the east and then north again to Cambridge street. From Cambridge street to Olive Street (now Mt. Vernon). It was called Hancock Street in 1788.

HANCOCK STREET: Removed by extension of the statehouse grounds in 1917. In 1788, it ran from Cambridge Street to Mt. Vernon Street. It was called George Street, Davis Lane and Turner Street at some time previous to 1732, when it ran from Beacon Street in the Common past Governor John Hancock's house, running northward over the hill from his garden down to Cambridge Street.

JOY STREET: Originally Zacheus Bosworth's passageway to his pastures.[141] It was accepted in 1851 from Beacon Street to Cambridge Street. The part from Cambridge Street to May Street (now Myrtle) was called Belknap's Lane (laid out in Mrs. Belknap's portion of land originally owned as ropewalk by Nathaniel Belknap) in 1787. It was called Belknap Street in 1789 and was extended south to Beacon Street through Clapboard Street (now Joy Street) and George Street (later Hancock Street) in 1803. Belknap Street between Myrtle and Beacon Street was called Joy Street in January 1851. The name was changed from Belknap to Joy by Cornelius Coolidge, architect and builder.

MESSENGER STREET: See Brimmer Street.

MIDDLECOTT STREET: See Bowdoin Street.

MT. VERNON STREET, 1832: From the easterly line of Hancock Street to the Charles River Embankment. It formerly ran from Beacon Street north and then west to the Charles River and from Beacon Street to the head of the former Temple Street, now Centry Street. From Beacon Street "round the new State House," it was called Sumner Street.

OLIVE STREET: North of John Joy's to the water, 1796. It ran from Belknap (now Joy) Street to Charles Street in 1817. Sumner Street extended through Olive Street on July 6, 1824. It was named Mt. Vernon Street on August 27, 1832.

OTTER STREET: From 99 Beacon Street to the Charles River Embankment. It formerly ran from 99 Beacon Street northerly to the Charles River, as shown on a plan by Alexander Wadsworth dated November 8, 1847. It was removed for the Storrow Drive entrance in 1950.

PARK STREET, 1803: From Tremont to Beacon Street. Named Park Street in 1803, also called Park Place. Its name was confirmed and accepted as a public street (Park Street) on September 15, 1834. Park Street extended to Mt. Vernon Street when the statehouse expansion in 1917 removed that extension. It was previously named Sumner Street, Temple Street and Mt. Vernon Street. See Sentry Street.

RIVER STREET: Today runs from Beacon north toward Pinckney Street. It was laid out in the 1833 plan of the MVP as Vermont Street.

SCHOOL STREET: From Washington Street to Tremont Street. It ran from Cornhill (now Washington Street) west across the Common (now Tremont Street) to the head of the present Somerset Street in 1708. An order was introduced on August 20, 1660, to extend School Street (named after the Boston Latin School, which originally was on the site of the present Old City Hall) with a view of providing a promenade to Centry Hill. Robert Turner, the leading caterer of the day, built near where the Bellevue now stands, in line of the direct extension to Beacon Hill. He therefore caused the street to be deflected to the Common and gave, in 1789, to the town the portion of Mt. Vernon Street that has recently (1917) been seized by the Commonwealth of Massachusetts, thus forming a way from the Common to Beacon Hill, called South Latin School Street.

SENTRY STREET, 1708: From Beacon Street up Centry Hill to the head of the present Temple Street; formerly called Centry or Sentry Street, which ran from Beacon Street north—"the way leading from Beacon Street, between Capt. Alford's land and Madame Shrimpton's pasture," up to Centry Hill (Beacon Hill, the summit of which is now memorialized by the Bulfinch column behind the statehouse) and Centry Street (called Century Street in 1732). It ran from Common Street (Tremont Street) to Beacon Hill in 1784 and from the Old Granary to the Old Almshouse in 1800. It was called Sumner Street (now Mt. Vernon) in 1800. The part from Common Street to Beacon Street was named Park Street in 1803.

SOMERSET STREET: First named in 1803. It ran from Beacon Street to Howard Street (formerly Southack's Court) and was laid out by John Bowers of Somerset, Massachusetts (hence the name).

SPRUCE STREET: From Beacon Street opposite the Common to Chestnut Street in 1822. It was confirmed as a public street on September, 15, 1834.

SUMNER STREET: Name changed in 1832 to Mt. Vernon. See Mt. Vernon Street.

TREMONT PLACE: First named in 1829. It ran from 4 Beacon Street south to the Granary Burying Ground.

TREMONT STREET, 1798: The portion from Pemberton Square to Beacon Street was called "the old burying place highway" in 1706. It was named Tramount Street by the town in 1708. After the naming of this portion, the street at various times was called Tramount, Tremount, Treamount and Trimount Street. It was also Common Street and finally Tremont Street.

VERMONT STREET: see River Street.

WALNUT STREET: Named in 1799, it ran from 38 Beacon Street to 38 Mt. Vernon Street. The easterly half was called Coventry Street from 1733 to 1791. It ran from Beacon Street to Olive (now Mt. Vernon) Street and was confirmed as a public street on June 19, 1834. Part of the street was at one time called Bishop Stokes Street.

Notes

Introduction

1. Records of the Court of Assistants, September 17, 1630. Winsor, *Memorial History*, vol. 1., 116.

Chapter 1

2. There is considerable debate about the exact year Blackstone settled in Boston. Bowditch, in his Gleaner articles, puts it at 1623, as does Drake in *History and Antiquities*, but a later date is more reasonable given the departure dates of Gorges and Morrell and the probability that Blackstone would have remained at Wessagusset until after their departures.
3. Gleaner, 6.
4. Gardner, *Settlers Around Boston Bay*.
5. Drake, *History and Antiquities*, 95, 95fn.
6. Ibid., 530. See also Gleaner, 189.
7. Gleaner, 2.

Chapter 2

8. Shurtleff, *Topographical Description*, 170.
9. Sentry Hill (also spelled Centry).
10. Wheildon, *Sentry Hill*, 10.
11. "It is ordered that there shal be forth with a beacon sett on the centry hill at Boston, to give notice to the country of any danger." General Court of the Colony.
12. Six square rods was approximately 182 square yards.

CHAPTER 3

13. Gleaner, 96.
14. Ibid., 96.
15. *Boston Evening Record,* January 4, 1888.
16. Forbes, *Other Statues*, 25.
17. Bacon, *King's Dictionary*, 455.

CHAPTER 4

18. Gleaner, 108.
19. Chamberlain, *Beacon Hill*, 49.
20. Winsor, *Memorial History*, vol. 2, 522.
21. Ibid., 521.
22. Gleaner, 108.
23. *Beacon Hill Times*, December 1, 1998, 14.
24. Boston Landmarks Commission Report.
25. Bacon, *King's Dictionary*, 87.

CHAPTER 5

26. The First Church is now located at the corner of Marlborough and Berkeley Streets.
27. Thwing, *Crooked and Narrow*, 144.
28. The Granary Burial Ground was first known as the South Burial Ground and was created from land of the Common. Copp's Hill was known as the North Burial Ground.
29. Kay, *Lost Boston*, 138.
30. O'Connor, *Civil War Boston*, 3.
31. Boston Landmarks Commission Report, Area CBD.
32. Fifty Associates still exists today.
33. Bowen, *Yankee From Olympus*, 267.
34. Slautterback, *Boston Athenaeum*, 60.
35. Ibid.
36. I visually inspected this building in May 2001 as it was undergoing partial conversion to residences.
37. Crawford, *Famous Families*, vol. 2, 149.
38. Johnson, *Seven and Eight Park*, 7.
39. Crawford, *Famous Families*, 127fn.
40. Ibid., vol. 2, 154.

CHAPTER 6

41. Drake, *Landmarks*, 282.
42. Crawford, *Famous Families*, vol. 1, 14.
43. Gleaner, 128.
44. Holmes, *Autocrat*, 125.
45. Holleran, *Boston's Changeful Times*, 188–93.
46. Means, *Old Park Street*, 18.
47. *Old Time New England* 27, 19.
48. Ibid., vol. 17, 6.
49. Drake, *Old Landmarks*, 338.
50. Gleaner, 158.
51. *Old Time New England* 17, advertisement for John Hancock Insurance Co.
52. New York State Historical Association, *Proceedings of the Twenty-sixth Annual Meeting*, 285.
53. Bowen, *Yankee from Olympus*, 119.
54. Chamberlain, *Beacon Hill*, 156.
55. Curtis, *Campestris Ulm*, 70fn.
56. City of Boston Council Records 1824, vol. 2. "C. Coolidge states he is about to start building at the corner of Beacon and Belknap (Joy) Streets."

CHAPTER 7

57. Winsor, *Memorial History*, vol. 4, 65.
58. *Mayors of Boston*, 14; Winsor, *Memorial History*, vol. 4, 65.
59. Gleaner, 53.
60. Tharp, *The Appletons*, 83.
61. Ibid., 88.
62. *Boston Almanac of 1883*, 79.
63. *1928 Clarke's Blue Book*.
64. Chamberlain, *Beacon Hill*, 126.

CHAPTER 8

65. The high water mark of the Charles River or the "beach," as it was known, is today at Sixty-two Beacon Street.
66. *Suffolk County Registry of Deeds*, Book 182, 186.

CHAPTER 9

67. Bullfinch Deposition re: Filling of Charles Street, 413/27.
68. Morison, *Harrison Gray Otis*, 219.
69. Crawford, *Famous Families*, 209.
70. Drake, *Historic Mansions*, 27.

71. This road was named the Mill Dam Road and was soon renamed Western Avenue; it later became Beacon Street (extension).

Chapter 10

72. Boston had never been incorporated as a town, so the 1822 creation of the city of Boston was the first corporation established. The legal inhabitants of the town approved the legislature's granting of a city charter in a referendum vote on March 22, 1822. Winsor, *Memorial History*, vol. 3, 218.
73. Morison, *Harrison Gray Otis*, 460.
74. These were the Upper Copley House, Lower Copley House and a smaller nondescript house.
75. Williams, *Greater Boston Clubs*, 85.
76. Tharp, *Appletons of Beacon Hill*, 105.
77. Marqus, *Jackson*.
78. Gleaner, 210.
79. Ibid.
80. Drake, *Old Landmarks*, 336.
81. Zimmer, *Old Time New England*, vol. 70, 99.
82. Winthrop, *Sears Memoir*.
83. Person, *Tocqueville and Beaumont*, 364.
84. Whitehill and Whitehill, *Somerset Club*, 21.
85. Gleaner, 211.
86. Morison, *Harrison Gray Otis*, 519.
87. Adams, *Boston Money Tree*, 205.
88. Person, *Tocqueville and Beaumont*.
89. Morison, *Harrison Gray Otis*, 434, 455.
90. Ibid., 547.
91. *Bulletin of the American Meteorological Society* 41, no. 9 (September 1960): 507–16.
92. Shand-Tucci, *Built in Boston*, 80.
93. Williams, *Greater Boston Clubs*, 85.
94. Greenslet, *The Lowells*, 211.
95. Baker, *Richard Morris Hunt*, 228.
96. Chamberlain, *Beacon Hill*, 171.
97. Seasholes, *Gaining Ground*, 356.
98. State Street Bank & Trust, *Other Statues of Boston*, 40. See also note in Williams, *Greater Boston Clubs*, 17.
99. www.sah.org.
100. www.LowellObservatory.edu.

Chapter 11

101. Morison, *Harrison Gray Otis*, 484.
102. Williams, *Greater Boston Clubs*, 29.

103. Tharp, *The Appletons*, 277.
104. *The Cathedral Church of St. Paul*, brochure describing history of the church.
105. Tharp, *The Appletons*, 295.
106. Ibid., 296.
107. Crawford, *Famous Families*, vol. 2, 184fn.
108. *Antiques*, December 1999.
109. Crawford, *Famous Families*, vol. 1, 120.
110. Gleaner, 221.
111. Crawford, *Famous Families*, vol. 2, 69.
112. Zimmer, *Old Time New England*, vol. 17, no. 1, xiii.
113. Gleaner, 202.
114. Adams, *Boston Money Tree*, 136.
115. Gleaner, 221.
116. Holleran, *Boston's Changeful Times.*

Chapter 12

117. Friends of the Public Garden, *Public Garden*, 8.
118. Crawford, *Famous Families*, vol. 2, 311.
119. Friends of the Public Garden, *Public Garden*, 8.
120. Ibid., 16.
121. Winsor, *Memorial History*, vol. 4, 32.
122. Gleaner, 75.

Chapter 13

123. Morison, *Harrison Gray Otis*, 221.
124. Crawford, *Famous Families*, vol. 2, 64.
125. Ibid., 85.
126. "A First-Person Account by Walter Scott Fitz of His Remarkable 36-Day Transcontinental Journey," Central Pacific Railroad Photographic Museum, http://cprr.org.
127. Crawford, *Famous Families*, vol. 2, 298.
128. Hill, *Historical Register.*
129. Ibid., 185.
130. "History of the Hampshire House," www.hampshirehouse.com/history.

Chapter 14

131. Crawford, *Famous Families*, vol. 2, 362.

CHAPTER 15

132. Bunting, *Houses of Back Bay*, 53.
133. Shand-Tucci, *Built in Boston*, 51.

APPENDIX A

134. *Second Report of the Record Commissioners of the City of Boston 1881*, Part II, 3.
135. Boston City Council Records, 1824, vol. 2, 210.

APPENDIX B

136. Boston Town Records, March 30, 1640.
137. Shurtleff, *Topographical and Historical Description*, 308.
138. City of Boston, *Nomenclature of Streets, 1879*, 17, appendix A.
139. Gleaner, 31.
140. Street Laying Out Department, *Record of Streets* (City of Boston, 1902), 32.
141. Gleaner, 163.

BIBLIOGRAPHY

Adams, Charles Francis. *Old Planters About Boston Harbor.* Massachusetts Historical Society, 1878.

————. *Three Episodes in Massachusetts History.* Boston: Houghton Mifflin, 1894.

Adams, Russell B., Jr. *The Boston Money Tree.* New York: Thomas Y. Crowell, 1977.

Allan, Herbert S. *John Hancock: Patriot in Purple.* New York: The Beechhurst Press, 1953.

Amory, Cleveland. *The Proper Bostonians.* New York: E.P. Dutton, 1947.

Amory, Martha Babcock. *John Singleton Copley.* Boston: Houghton Mifflin, 1882.

Andrews, Charles M. *Colonial Period of American History.* 4 vols. New Haven: Yale University Press, 1936.

Ayer, Mary Farwell. *Boston Common in Colonial and Provincial Days.* Boston: Merrymount Press, 1903.

————. *Early Days on Boston Common.* Boston: Merrymount Press, 1910.

Bacon, Edwin M. *King's Dictionary of Boston.* Boston: Moses King Publishing Co., 1883.

Baker, Paul R. *Richard Morris Hunt.* Cambridge, MA: MIT Press, 1986.

Ballou, Hosea Starr. *William Blaxton: The First Bostonian.* Bostonian Society Proceedings, 1931–35.

Banner, James M., Jr. *To the Hartford Convention.* New York: Alfred A. Knopf, 1970.

Bergen, Philip, ed. *Old Boston in Early Photos, 1850–1918.* Boston: Dover Publications, 1990.

Boston's Growth. State Street Bank and Trust Co., 1910.

Bowen, Catherine Drinker. *Yankee From Olympus.* Boston: Little Brown & Co., 1944.

Bunting, Bainbridge. *Houses of Boston's Back Bay, 1840–1917.* Cambridge: Belknap Press, 1967.

Carruth, Frances Weston. *Fictional Rambles About Boston.* New York: McClure Phillips & Co., 1902.

Chamberlain, Allen. *Beacon Hill, Its Ancient Pastures.* Boston: Houghton Mifflin, 1925.

Change and Continuity: Photos of the Boston Athenaeum. Boston Athenaeum, n.d.

Clark, Edward E, ed. *Clark's Blue Book.* Boston: Sampson & Murdock Co., 1876, 1891, 1928, 1934.

Commonwealth of Massachusetts. *Bulfinch State House Centennial.* Boston, 1898.

———. *Historical Data of Towns of Massachusetts.* Boston, 1997.

Conwell, Colonel P.H. *History of the Great Fire in Boston.* Boston: Russell Publishing, 1873.

Crawford, Mary C. *Famous Families of Massachusetts.* 2 vols. Boston: Little Brown & Co., 1930.

———. *Old Boston Days and Ways.* Boston: Little Brown & Co., 1909.

———. *Romantic Days in Old Boston.* Boston: Little, Brown & Co., 1922.

Curtis, Joseph Henry. *Life of Campestris Elm.* Boston: W.B. Clarke Co., 1910.

Drake, Samuel A. *Historic Mansions & Highways Around Boston.* Boston. Little Brown & Co., 1906.

———. *Old Landmarks and Historic Personages of Boston.* Boston: Little Brown & Co., 1906.

Drake, Samuel G. *History and Antiquities of Boston.* Boston: Luther Stevens, 1856.

Egleston, Melville. *The Land Systems of the New England Colonies.* Baltimore, MD: John Hopkins University Press, 1886.

Felt, Joseph B. *Who Was the First Governor of Massachusetts.* Boston: T.R. Marvin Press, 1853.

Flick, Alexander C. *John Hancock's House.* New York State Historical Association, Twenty-eight Annual Meeting, 1926.

Forbes, Allan. *Boston England & Boston New England.* Boston: State Street Bank & Trust, 1930.

———. *Other Statues of Boston.* Boston: State Street Trust Co., 1947.

Forty of Boston's Historic Houses. Pamphlet monograph. State Street Trust Co., 1912.

Fowler, William M., Jr. *The Baron of Beacon Hill.* Boston: Houghton Mifflin, 1980.

Fox, Pamela. " Nathan Appleton's Beacon St. Houses." *Old Time New England* 70 (1980): 111–23.

Frost, Jack, and G. Stinson Lord, eds. *Two Forts...to Destiny.* North Scituate, MA: Hawthorne Press, 1971.

Gardner, L.M. *Settlers Around Boston Bay Prior to 1630.* Salem, MA: Salem Press, 1910.

Greenslet, Ferris. *The Lowell and Their Seven Worlds.* Boston: Houghton Mifflin, 1946.

Hale, Edward E., ed. *Notebook of Thomas Lechford, Esq., 1638–1641.* Cambridge, MA: John Wilson, 1885.

Harris, John. *Historical Walks in Old Boston.* Boston: Globe Pequot Press, 1982.

Hart, Robert Bushnell. *Commonwealth History of Massachusetts.* 5 vols. New York State History Company, 1927.

Haven, Samuel F. *History of Grants under the Council of New England.* Massachusetts Historical Society, 1869.

Hill, Edwin Charles. *The Historical Register, 1921.* New York: Edwin C. Hill, 1920.

Holleran, Michael. *Boston's Changeful Times.* Baltimore, MD: John Hopkins University Press, 1998.

Holmes, Oliver Wendell. *The Autocrat of the Breakfast Table.* Boston: Houghton Mifflin, 1894.

Homer, Rachel J., ed. *Legacy of Josiah Johnson Hawes.* Barre, MA: Barre Publishers, 1972.

Howe, Daniel W. *The Puritan Republic.* Indianapolis, IN: The Bowen-Merrill Co., 1899.

Howe, M.A. DeWolfe. *Boston Common Scenes from Four Centuries.* Boston: Atlantic Monthly Press, 1921.

BIBLIOGRAPHY

Hutchinson, Thomas. *History of the Province of Massachusetts Bay, 1691–1750*. London: J. Smith, 1767.

"Johns S. Copley's Houses on Beacon Hill." *Old Time New England* 25 (1935): 85–95.

Johnson, R B. *Seven & Eight Park Street*. Boston: Thomas Todd, 1976.

Kay, Jane Holtz. *Lost Boston*. Boston: Houghton Mifflin, 1980.

Kershaw, Gordon E. *James Bowdoin II*. Lanham, MD: University Press of America, 1991.

King, Moses. *King's Handbook of Boston*. Boston: Moses King, 1878.

Kirker, Harold, and James Kirker. *Bulfinch's Boston*. New York: Oxford University Press, 1964.

Krieger, A., and D. Cobb, ed. *Mapping Boston*. Cambridge: MIT Press, 1999.

Kyle, George A. *The Eighteen Fifties*. Boston: Boston 5¢ Savings Bank, 1926.

Lawrence, Robert Means. *Old Park Street & Vicinity*. Boston: Houghton Mifflin, 1922.

Lind, Louise. *William Blackstone: Sage of the Wilderness*. Bowie, MD: Heritage Books, 1993.

Loring, James Spear, ed. *One Hundred Boston Orators*. Boston: John Jewett & Co., 1852.

Lyndon, Donlyn. *The City Observed*. New York: Vintage Books, 1982.

Mayo, Lawrence Shaw, ed. *The History of the Colony and Province of Massachusetts Bay*. Cambridge, MA: Harvard University Press, 1936.

Mayors of Boston. Boston: State Street Trust Co., 1914.

McIntyre, A. McVoy. *Beacon Hill: A Walking Tour*. Boston: Little, Brown & Co., 1975.

Morison, Samuel Eliot. *Builders of the Bay Colony*. Boston: Houghton Mifflin, 1930.

———. *European Discoveries of American North Voyages*. New York: Oxford University Press, 1971.

———. *Harrison Gray Otis*. Boston: Houghton Mifflin, 1969.

———. *Harrison Gray Otis*. 2 vols. Boston: Houghton Mifflin, 1913.

———. *One Boy's Boston*. Cambridge: Riverside Press, 1962.

Morse, J.M. "Division of Land by the Council of New England in 1623." *New England Quarterly* 7, no. 3 (1935).

Mount, Charles Merrill. *Gilbert Stuart, A Biography*. New York: W.W. Norton & Co, 1964.

Mr. Bulfinch's Boston. Boston: Old Colony Trust, 1963.

O'Connor, Thomas H. *Civil War Boston*. Boston: Northeastern University Press, 1997.

"Parker-Inches-Emery House." *Old Time New England* 9 (1913): 2–11.

Person, George W. *Tocqueville & Beaumont in America*. New York: Oxford Press, 1938.

Pomfret, John E. *Founding the American Colonies, 1583–1660*. New York: Harper & Row, 1971.

Preston, Richard Arthur. *Gorges of Plymouth Fort*. Toronto, ON: University of Toronto Press, 1953.

Public Garden [Boston]. *Friends of the Public Garden and Common*. 1988.

Quincy, Josiah. *Municipal History of the City of Boston*. Boston: Little & Brown, 1852.

Rebora, C. "John Singleton Copley's Houses." *American Art Journal* 27 (n.d.).

Rutman, Darrett B. *Winthrop's Boston*. New York: W.W. Norton Co., 1965.

Seaburg, Carl. *Boston Observed*. Boston: Beacon Press, 1971.

Seasholes, Nancy S. *Gaining Ground.* Cambridge: MIT Press, 2003.

Shand-Tucci, Douglass. *Built in Boston, City & Suburb 1800–1950.* Amherst: University of Massachusetts Press, 1978.

Shurtleff, Nathaniel B. *Topographical Description of Boston.* Boston: A. Williams & Co., 1871.

Slautterback, Catharina. *Designing the Boston Athenaeum.* Boston: Boston Athenaeum, 1999.

Some Interesting Boston Events. Boston: State Street Trust Co., 1916.

Some Statues of Boston. Boston: State Street Trust Co., 1946.

Spring, James W. *Boston and the Parker House.* Boston: J.R. Whipple Corp., 1927.

Stout, Harry S. *The New England Soul.* New York: Oxford University Press, 1986.

Suffolk Deeds Liber XI 1678–1680. Boston: Rockwell & Churchill 1900.

Suffolk Deeds Liber XII 1680–1683. Boston: Rockwell & Churchill 1902.

Sullivan, James. *Land Titles in Massachusetts.* Boston: I. Thomas & E.T. Andrews, 1801.

Tharp, Louise Hall. *The Appletons of Beacon Hill.* Boston: Little Brown & Co., 1973.

Thwing, Annie H. *Crooked and Narrow Streets of Boston.* Boston: Charles E. Lauriat, 1930.

Unger, Harlow Giles. *John Hancock.* New York: John Wiley & Sons, 2000.

Wanderwarker, Peter. *Boston Then and Now.* New York: Dover Publishing, 1982.

Watkins, Walter Kendall. "The Hancock House & Its Builder." *Old Time New England* 17 (1926): 3–20.

Weinhardt, Carl J., Jr. *Domestic Architecture of Beacon Hill.* Boston: Bostonian Society, 1958.

Wheildon, William W. *Beacon or Sentry Hill.* Boston: Rand Avery & Co., 1877.

Whitehill, Walter Muir. *Boston, A Topographical History.* Cambridge, MA: Belknap Press, 1959.

Whitehill, William, and Whitney Whitehill. *The Somerset Club, 1851–1951.* Boston: Anthoensen Press, 1951.

Whitmore, W.H., ed. *Record Commissioners Reports.* City of Boston, 1876–1909.

Williams, Alexander W. *Social History of the Greater Boston Clubs.* Barre, MA: Barre Publishing, 1970.

Winslow, Elizabeth. *Samuel Sewall of Boston.* New York: Macmillan Co., 1964.

Winsor, Justin, ed. *Memorial History of Boston, 1630–1880.* 4 vols. Boston: Ticknor & Co., 1880.

Winthrop, John. *History of New England, 1630–49.* 2 vols. Boston: Little Brown & Co., 1853.

Winthrop, Robert C., Jr. *Memoir of the Hon. David Sears.* Cambridge, MA: John Wilson & Son, University Press, 1886.

Young, Alexander. *Chronicles of the First Planters of Massachusetts Bay.* Boston: Charles C. Little, 1846.

Zimmer, Edward F. "Alexander Parris–David Sears House." *Old Time New England* 70 (1980): 99–109.